TO BE A MARMA

Dr Farhana Hoque

TO BE A MARMA

A passionately lived identity on the borderlands between Bangladesh and Myanmar

The Anthropology Collection

Editor
Dr Janise Hurtig

First published in 2022 by Lived Places Publishing

All rights reserved. No part of this publication may be reproduced, stored in a retrieval system, or transmitted in any form or by any means, electronic, mechanical, photocopying, recording or otherwise, without prior permission in writing from the publisher.

The author and editors have made every effort to ensure the accuracy of information contained in this publication, but assume no responsibility for any errors, inaccuracies, inconsistencies and omissions. Likewise, every effort has been made to contact copyright holders. If any copyright material has been reproduced unwittingly and without permission the Publisher will gladly receive information enabling them to rectify any error or omission in subsequent editions.

Copyright © 2022 Lived Places Publishing

British Library Cataloguing in Publication Data
A CIP record for this book is available from the British Library

ISBN: 9781915271181 (pbk)
ISBN: 9781915271204 (ePDF)
ISBN: 9781915271198 (ePUB)

The right of Farhana Hoque to be identified as the Author of this work has been asserted by her in accordance with the Copyright, Design and Patents Act 1988.

Cover design by Fiachra McCarthy
Book design by Rachel Trolove of Twin Trail Design
Typeset by Newgen Publishing UK

Lived Places Publishing
Long Island
New York 11789
www.livedplacespublishing.com

For Sami and Hana

Abstract

The book explores a passionately lived identity on the borderlands between South and Southeast Asia. It focusses on one ethnic group, the Marma of the Chittagong Hill Tracts. The book places the everyday lives and meanings of a remote hill people at the heart of a study on identity and nothing is taken for granted. By looking at the history of the region and the way it has shaped the Marma, as well as an analysis of ethnographic data, the book establishes the nature of the group's cultural distinctness. Themes covered are Marma marriage customs and rituals, oral histories around migration and settlement, and Marma material culture and ceremonials.

Keywords

Marma; Chittagong Hill Tracts; Bangladesh; Buddhism; Burma/Myanmar; ethnic identity; invention of culture; hybridity; syncretism; entanglement; borderlands; migration; Zomia

Contents

Acknowledgements — ix

Introduction — 1

Chapter 1 Teacher and student guide — 15
- **Learning objectives** — 15
- **Learner objectives** — 15
- **Suggested activities (general)** — 16
- **Suggested activities (by chapter)** — 16
- **Recommended projects** — 17

Chapter 2 The project and the people — 19

Chapter 3 A toolkit to study identity on the borderlands: a brief summary — 35

Chapter 4 Marma kinship and marriage rituals — 43

Chapter 5 Ethnic endogamy: land, culture, and religion — 79

Chapter 6 Migration and settlement — 101

Chapter 7 The invention of Marma material culture and ceremonials — 137

Conclusions — 163

Notes — 172

References — 189

Recommended further reading	197
Glossary	200
Appendix A Introductions and experts in the Marma community	210
Appendix B Historical timeline	214
Appendix C A toolkit to study identity on the borderlands	216
Appendix D Royal chart and new genogram	244
Appendix E Map of Bandarban with shrines	246
Appendix F Documentary – To be a Marma	249
Index	251

Acknowledgements

The ethnographic research was initially made possible thanks to the help of Professor Willem Van Schendel, who is an expert on Asian borderlands. My special thanks go to Shai Shing Aung, his family – including his monk grandfather – and his musical circle of friends for incorporating me into the spiritual and joyful rhythms of their lives. I am extremely grateful for getting to know Daisy, Lobu, and Dauki, and that we became good friends. And to Jerry Allen – honorary Khyang by marriage – for sharing his photos from the *raj punya* of the 15th Bohmong.

My gratitude to my Bangladeshi aunts and cousins in Dhaka and Chittagong for stopovers, meals, and laughter. And to my mother – Amina Chowdhury – who accompanied me on the first trip, navigating a very challenging country that was different to the country she left behind in 1971. To Fiona Kerlogue (Horniman Museum) and Ed Owles (Postcode Films) for the exciting projects around material culture and film that helped to make the Marma narrative take on another life beyond the written word.

Back home in London, I am indebted to my supervisors at University College London – Dr Allen Abramson and Professor Roland Littlewood – for their invaluable guidance, energy, and support during the long journey of completing my PhD, on which this book is based.

Introduction

In the last 30 years, borderlands all over the world have been part of the political and academic debates around globalisation, migration, and security. In Europe, for example, the expansion of the European Union, the collapse of the Soviet bloc, the shaping of new nations, and the mass movement of peoples from east to west and south to north are but some of the factors that have not only transformed borders in Europe but also stimulated new kinds of scholarship around it.

Anthropologists have been part of these debates, but specifically looking at the cultural effects of globalisation and migration on border communities. Some border studies also try to understand how ethnic groups negotiate their identity alongside other cultures that express similar or different notions of being and belonging on the borderlands.

This book is a contribution to border studies and identity. It focuses on a region called the Chittagong Hill Tracts (CHT), which straddles the borders between Bangladesh and Myanmar. This region has experienced many different groups migrating to the area and has been governed over a period of approximately 500 years by an impressive line-up of local and global powers – the Arakan kingdom, the Portuguese, the Mughals, and the British Empire. This book is an exploration of the identity of one ethnic group – the Marma – who live in this historically complex and fluid region of the world.

The stories and thoughts you will find in this book are based on the fieldwork in the Marma community that was part of my PhD research at University College London. This fieldwork was conducted between November 2012 and December 2014, in Bandarban town in the CHT.

Meet the Marma

I was born in Bangladesh, or East Pakistan as it was then, and my family left the region towards the end of Bangladesh's War of Independence in 1971.[1] In 2012, I returned to the CHT in Bangladesh for the first time in 20 years to begin the fieldwork.

On a previous visit to the CHT in 1993, I had travelled the country on holiday as a young adult and met for the first time the Chakma people in and around Rangamati in the CHT. The area was off-limits to foreigners, but as a Bangladesh-born citizen I was able to travel the area unhindered. What struck me then was the contrast with "mainland" Bangladesh, with its expansive, flat delta and densely populated towns and cities. The CHT, in sharp contrast, was sparsely populated. There were at the time 15 ethnic groups living in small rural towns and villages scattered across this hilly jungle landscape. Moreover, the people in the hill tracts looked, dressed, and acted differently to the Bangladeshis that I had encountered.

Returning in 2012, the contrast was, if anything, even greater. Departing from Chittagong, by then the second-largest city in Bangladesh with a population of circa 4 million, I travelled to Bandarban town in the CHT, which had a population of approximately 32,000. In and around Bandarban town, alongside the numerous mosques calling Bengali Muslims to prayer, stood several Arakan-style[2] royal palaces built by various Bohmong *Rajas* – chiefs or kings of the Marma people – and an impressive Golden Buddhist temple. My first impressions of Bandarban were not that different from a description of the community noted in 1927:

> To one who has become used to the Bengali atmosphere of the Chakma and Mong circles, to visit Bandarban, the headquarters of the Bohmong, is to enter a new world. It is pure Burma, with yellow-robed priests, Bhuddhist temples and a populace clad in Burmese dress of all the colours of the rainbow. There Bengali culture is disdained as something alien, and all regard Burma as their spiritual home. This clear-cut and striking difference between the Bohmong's circle and those of the Chakma Chief and the Mong *Raja* cannot be too strongly emphasized.
>
> (Mills, 1927, p. 75)

When staying with a Marma family in a compound of five households, I experienced even more interesting juxtapositions. This Marma family spoke fluent Bengali[3] to non-Marma visitors, so it seemed that Bengali had become the lingua franca of the region. They spoke Marma to each other, a language that has a written script which mostly the elder members of the family know how to read. The family loosely followed Bengali eating customs and mealtimes, but the content of the food was very different to a typical Bengali meal: fried strips of wild boar, river oysters, bamboo shoots, and many soupy cabbage dishes. There was a photo of the prime minister of Bangladesh – Sheikh Hasina[4] – in their communal rooms. However, tucked away in the most private rooms of their homes was a family Buddhist shrine.

The Marma dress style was Burmese in origin and the envy of the other ethnic groups of the CHT, who seem to have either adopted Bengali clothes – a *sari* or *shalwar kameez* – or tribal renditions of Bengali-style clothing. I came to learn that Marma practise ethnic endogamy: a custom of marrying within the limits of the clan or ethnic group. Intermarriage with tribal groups, if they were Buddhist, was tolerated. However, a Muslim marriage partner was frowned upon. I was also informed of the most recent scandal in the royal family: the daughter of the Bohmong *Raja* (King) had married a local Bangladeshi Muslim who was an officer in the Bangladeshi army. There were riots and protests against the marriage, but the Bohmong *Raja* ultimately stood by his daughter's decision. It felt like here on this narrow strip of hilly land between Muslim Bangladesh and Buddhist Myanmar, people were experiencing something similar to a clash of civilisations.

I was fascinated by the Marma people. Specifically, how they appeared to maintain a singular cultural heritage while living alongside different ethnic groups in a majority culture that was very different to theirs. They appeared to live their identity fully and with a passion, and their cultural journey seemed to underscore this.

The next sections will walk the reader through the various steps involved in the fieldwork on the Marma community and highlight the key themes of the book.

Ethnic hybridity

During this first visit to Bandarban, I repeatedly heard about the fascinating history of the Marma community, both from oral history accounts and from a huge Bohmong family genealogy chart that stood as a museum object at the entrance of the local Tribal Cultural Institute in Bandarban town. When I came back to London, I checked the Marma narratives against the historical reports of J. P. Mills (1927, 1931) to the British Government concerning the CHT, archived in the India Office Records at the British Library. I discovered that Marma oral history was also recorded history in these official documents.

As part of this historical account, I observed that the Marma group are Buddhist but were originally made up of different ethnicities from Burma – Burmese, Mon, and Arakan – who, through various waves of migration, had settled in the Bandarban district to be ruled by a long line of Bohmong chiefs. The Marma people are therefore an ethnically hybrid group. Within the group, people share common values, eating customs, marriage rules, and religion, and they speak dialects of the same language.

Yet what was particularly striking was that, despite this ethnic hybridity, the group gave the impression of having a singular identity, which is why they stood out as a unique community in the region.

Little Burma

There are over three royal circles in the CHT, and the number of ethnic groups is now 11, as opposed to the 15 communities of the early 1990s. These ethnic communities are collectively seen – by the Bangladeshi state, which is predominantly Muslim – as a non-Muslim buffer zone to Buddhist Myanmar and Hindu India.

The Marma are the second-largest minority group in the CHT and they live mainly in the Bohmong Circle but can also be found in the Chakma Circle (Rangamati area) and Mong Circle (Khagrachari), as well as the coastal areas of Cox's Bazar. The Bohmong Circle is widely claimed to be the most peaceful in the hill tracts. Local people put this down to the Golden Temple and three Buddhist pilgrimage sites in the district. These pilgrimage sites house sacred Buddha relics that were transported to this region during the migration from Pegu (now Bago) in Burma in the 1600s. Moreover, because of historical circumstances and the legacy of British protection, the Marma community in Bandarban have managed to maintain a system of governance that gives the district the appearance of a semi-independent kingdom. This, together with its reputation for peacefulness, has meant that the Bohmong Circle is referred to by Bangladeshis and other groups in the area as "Little Burma".

Shininess

Another key marker that differentiated the Marma from other ethnic groups in the CHT, as well the mainland Bangladeshis, was the bedazzling amount of gold or radiance in the landscape in which they lived. *Alan raung*[5] (the power of shininess) could be seen everywhere. From the huge structures of glittering golden *stupas* within and around Bandarban town, to specific sacred sculptures such as the golden bell hanging from a golden dragon at the largest Golden Temple. From the shininess of clothing and props around funerals of both revered Buddhist monks and senior members of the royal family, to the royal sword that is handed down from generation to generation of

Bohmong chiefs, with its glittering golden hilt; and the shininess of the coin garlands given to brides on their marriage day, to protect them during widowhood and divorce. Shininess seemed to represent something undetermined and yet significant for the Marma people. For example, it seemed to me that the Marma people embraced the concept of "shininess" to acknowledge three different things: the radiance of their Buddhist faith, the legitimating shine of the power of the royal family, and the protective shininess of bridal gifts.

Stability in flux

What was remarkable was that the Marma community appears to have responded to living on the borderlands by *not* assimilating to the dominant Bangladeshi group or to the mix of neighbouring cultures. Instead, the Marma people seem to have undergone a cultural process of distilling, revisiting, reproducing, renewing, and consolidating a Marma identity at the core of their cultural life. Unlike other ethnic communities in the CHT borderlands, the Marma community asserts its uniqueness through the persistent affirmation of various cultural practices and resources that seem to be rooted in the past. These core cultural practices seem to have been reproduced over time and continue to differentiate the group from the other groups in the region. It also explains why the ethnic community gives the impression of an eternal stable group in a region of extreme changeability and flux.

Climate change

For some time now, the CHT has been experiencing a crisis due to the run-on effects of climate change in Bangladesh as a whole. The rise in delta waters is resulting in the disappearance of cultivable alluvial soils in the lowlands of Bangladesh. With over 160 million people crammed into circa 150,000 square kilometres, Bangladesh is desperately short of land. Consequently, there has been a steady migration of the Bengali Muslim population to the higher lands of the CHT. This has had a huge impact on the CHT. After enjoying over 200 years of peaceful isolation on the borders, the CHT is now "overrun" by Bengali Muslims, and the minority groups that live there feel that their independence and access to land is under threat. Moreover, the rise in the number of Bengali Muslim settlers has resulted in the further militarisation of the area.[6] Because of this, at the time I was conducting my fieldwork with the Marma, there was a collective feeling of uncertainty about the future of the Marma community. The wealthier Marma families were planning to leave the area and return to Myanmar[7] or travel beyond the borders.

Studying a lived identity in the borderlands

This study will reveal how one ethnic minority, isolated and on the margins of mainstream culture, passionately live their identity in the borderlands.

This book employs ethnographic data that emerged from the observation of rituals and the narratives around material culture, as well as various theoretical tools that help to unpick the processes of cultural reproduction and constant reinvention in the Marma community. While some groups on borderlands become entangled and assimilate with other groups and the nation state, other groups work on their cultural boundaries to do the exact opposite. To both differentiate, demarcate, and, through these processes, achieve legitimacy and some freedom in an otherwise highly militarised and politicised zone.

The book presents various narratives, in the form of ethnographic data, around the Marma lived experience. The theory and academic framework serves as the lens to understand how these narratives contribute to the Marma identity as a whole. My main contention is that border communities and their identity negotiation "need to be taken as processes not givens, and the manner in which they are produced and made to appear as given needs to be studied critically" (Gellner, 2013, p. 5). Outside of ethnographic data and my fieldwork findings, I have referred to other descriptions of the community and the CHT that emerged from travellers to the area, both colonial emissaries and anthropologists. Moreover, to fully grasp the significance of the Marma identity in the CHT, I regularly compare the Bohmong Circle, where the Marma reside, with the other two circles in the CHT, as well as contrast the lived experience of the Marma with the largest ethnic group, the Chakma.

I drew upon a wealth of experts from the region – see Appendix A for a full description.

The research is of importance to students of sociology and anthropology as it will hopefully provide some ideas on how to develop an approach to studying the identity of ethnic minorities on the peripheries of the state and/or in complex regions of the world such as borderlands or understanding communities in multicultural settings in urban zones across the globe.

About me

Since I was born in Bangladesh, I did not require a visa or permission to carry out research in Bangladesh as a whole. However, I was required to inform the local police and the army about my plans and movements throughout the research period.[8]

It was not easy to gain the trust and acceptance of the community. For the Marma, being Bangladesh-born meant that, although I spoke very broken Bengali, I also represented the majority culture, which was historically seen to be oppressive to minorities on the borderlands. I was perceived by some as representing the state and therefore the Enemy. However, the people who came to know me understood that I had never lived in Bangladesh and that I had spent most of my life in the UK and Europe. Moreover, the world of East Pakistan – before Independence – was a time of peace and stability and seen by the Marma as a happier time. After independence, mainland Bangladesh experienced successive military rulers while the minorities on the borderlands suffered military occupation.[9] Overall, it appeared that the people I worked with had stepped over the uncomfortable fact that I was a Bengali Bangladeshi, believing instead – or choosing to believe instead – that I was one of the acceptable ones that left before independence and was therefore untainted by what had happened afterwards.

Interestingly, during my first visit to Bangladesh, the news was dominated by the trials of former perpetrators of the 1971 Bangladesh War of Independence. Many of my Marma informants would include me in the discussions around the trials as if I was also part of their cultural experience.[10] The biggest issue that I faced was the fact that I was born a Muslim. This appeared to be at the forefront of people's minds as I was offered on numerous occasions "the pork and *arrack* test". *Arrack* is locally brewed rice wine which is drunk on social and ritual occasions and the local pork was a rice-fattened wild boar. If I was truly not part of the majority enemy State, I would sit with the Marma and drink *arrack* and eat fried sweet boar. No Bengali Muslim would do this. This test emerged often in the company of both young and older members of the community and, since I am not a practising Muslim, I stepped up to the challenge. Moreover, when my family came to visit the region for the Sangrai Water Festival in April 2014 and for the wedding of one of my informants, the fact that my husband was Dutch also helped to counter the anxieties about my Bengali heritage. They had not seen an ethnically Bengali woman in a mixed marriage before.

There were some advantages in being a "cultural semi-insider" (Tsuda, 2015, pp. 14–17). I could speak and understand Bengali, but most importantly I could see what was Bengali and what was Marma in their cultural practice. For example, fried sweet pork aside, the Marma people had assimilated more Bengali food-eating patterns than they had probably realised. They ate at Bengali times which was late at night, the portions of rice were huge compared to their South Asian neighbours, and they ate with their hands – not with chopsticks or spoons as would be expected from a Burmese origin group. Dishes that they called Marma pitas (cakes) were Bengali pitas, as I had grown up with them in my own household. However, I was told with total conviction that they were local Marma traditions. It was interesting to note that, while rejecting all things Bengali Bangladeshi, some things Bengali had become part of the Marma cultural food script over time.

Even though I am Bengali born, the people of Bandarban greeted me as *Ang ley ma*, which means English lady. Some members of the 15th Bohmong family could speak English, but most were trained in "Bangladeshi medium" and could only speak Bengali and Marma. Those who knew English were pleased to practise their English with me.

In the very initial stages of the fieldwork, learning the Marma language, staying in a household (my Marma host in Bandarban), and employing a local field assistant helped me to get a foothold in the locality. Language learning was a key activity during the first six months of fieldwork. Although I was able to use broken Bengali to communicate in the CHT, I realised that speaking Bengali would not take me far enough. Most people understand Bengali, but women especially have difficulties in expressing themselves in this language and the Bengali they knew was often a local dialect of Bengali called Chittagonian. I worked on learning simple Marma terms so that I could take part in daily greetings and basic exchanges. It seemed that part of my initial acceptance into the community was due to the fact that I enjoyed wearing Marma clothes and made the effort to learn Marma phrases on a daily basis.

A note about terminologies

The term *pahari* is a Bengali word and roughly translates to "hill people" (Uddin, 2010). The term *adivasi* has also been employed in historical literature of the CHT, but the label also applies to non-Bengali communities living throughout South Asia. Furthermore, it roughly translates as "indigenous", a term which implies descendants of those peoples who were in a certain geographical location before other peoples. Due to ongoing disputes around the indigeneity of communities in the CHT and their ownership of land, I have deliberately avoided using this term. "Jumma" is still prevalent among political groups and organisations, but as with *adivasi*, it is a highly politicised term and therefore sensitive.

For these reasons, in this book I have referred to the collection of groups living in the CHT as "hill people" or "ethnic minorities", "ethnic groups" or "ethnic communities". All of these terms refer to both men and women as people living in the hill tracts of Chittagong. It takes into account the fact that they may have migrated to the hills or moved there from neighbouring hilly regions, and that the groups are a minority and different to the majority culture. With regards to the Marma, I have often referred to them as the Marma people. Note also that throughout this book "Burma" is often used to describe the neighbouring state of Myanmar.

1
Teacher and student guide

Learning objectives

- **To understand a Passionately Lived Identity.** This book offers an insight into how marginal groups, affected by dramatic change in the environment, are determined and purposeful when investing in a group identity in contested spaces of the world.
- **To learn about the role of identity in ethnic survival in areas of extreme change and fluidity.** The book demonstrates the power of storytelling through an anthropological lens as it deepens understanding, promotes awareness, and stimulates debate on issues around the most pressing global challenges to marginal groups of the world.

Learner objectives

- To study the history of a region to understand how communities respond differently to external influences and how these influences impact ethnic identity.
- To raise awareness of the impact of colonial history and recent effects of climate change on ethnic groups in the borderlands of the world.

- To demonstrate the importance of studying one community in great depth in order to understand the many different aspects of identity formation.
- To listen to the narratives of a group's history through various aspects of their lived experience.
- To illustrate the usefulness of employing anthropological theories to unpick identity creation and maintenance on both the boundaries of culture and from within culture.

Suggested activities (general)

- Looking at the history of the region and the recent effects of climate change: how is the Marma response different compared to the other ethnic groups in the region?
- Identity the key themes of Marma identity and how the group continue to invest in them.
- Who are the different agents adapting Marma identity or inventing it?
- To what extent is ethnic identity shaped by external factors and to what extent is it a self-making project?
- What are the benefits and limitations of community ethnography?

Suggested activities (by chapter)

Chapter 2 The project and the people

- Who are the key powers in the CHT?
- How have they shaped the region?

Chapter 4 Marma kinship and marriage rituals

- What do marriage rules and customs achieve?

- What key anxieties do marriage rituals address?

Chapter 5 Ethnic endogamy: land, culture, and religion

- What are the challenges that the community are facing?
- How are they responding to it?

Chapter 6 Migration and settlement

- What function do narratives on Marma migration and settlement achieve?
- Discuss the role of a historical timeline approach to studying group identity.

Chapter 7 The invention of Marma material culture and ceremonials

- What is the role of material culture in the group's identity and what does it achieve?
- What are the key themes embodied in the objects and ceremonies?

Recommended projects

Design a short ethnographical field trip to understand the cultural identity of one community.

- Consider how you will capture data on identity and which methods you will use.
- When in the field, keep a daily journal and reflect on your first insights and impressions from the fieldwork.
- Identify themes and respondents, and start collating possible questions to draw out further insights.
- Check archives and published books on the history of the

group. Think about how history has shaped the group's identity: what were the key events and who were the key agents/people?
- Return to the community with a list of open-ended questions.
- Write up your analysis.

2
The project and the people

> It just so happens that the upland border area we have chosen to call Zomia represents one of the world's longest-standing and largest refuges of populations who live in the shadow of states but who have not yet been fully incorporated.
>
> (Scott, 2009, p. 325)

Understanding a region, its history, and the influences on a society and its culture are important starting points for any studies on identity. In this chapter, we will learn about the CHT's long history of migration, governance by external powers, insurgencies, and instability. The region has been ruled by many different "foreign" states, who have defined and shaped the region. While the borderlands may look confusing and complex to colonisers and state officials, the hill peoples themselves are neither confused nor mystified about who they are, and how they experience their cultural separateness in these remote spaces.

First of all, some background to this region. The CHT region lies in the Asian borderlands that have been labelled the *Southeast Asian massif* (Michaud, 1997) and more recently *Zomia* (Van Schendel, 2002), which is the eastern part of the Asian massif.

The people who now reside there represent the various migrants that were either fleeing war, famine, epidemics, or slavery. They could also be exiled royal lineages and their entourages, or religious dissidents. These refugees and migrants have chosen the little-governed space of the hills to live beyond the control of the political centres that are largely situated in the lower plains.

This book is an exploration of the identity of one ethnic community – the Marma people – who live in the CHT, located in Zomia.

The people of the CHT

The CHT is in the south-eastern part of Bangladesh, next to India to the north and east, Myanmar to the south, and Chittagong district to the west. Geographically, as part of the Himalayan range, the CHT region comprises numerous hills, forests, and river valleys. This is in complete contrast to the low-lying alluvial plains of the rest of Bangladesh. The CHT area is inhabited by around 11 ethnic communities. Of these, the Chakma and Marma people are numerically dominant, living mainly in valley areas and practising both plough and swidden agriculture – locally known as *jhum* cultivation. The other groups of people, such as the Tripura, Bawm, Khumi, Lusai, Chak, and Mru, occupy the mountain areas and practise mainly swidden agriculture. The CHT borderlands expert Van Schendel observed that all groups throughout their history were continually on the move as swidden cultivators, but also because of raids and warfare (Van Schendel, 1992, pp. 99–100).

Nearly all the major regional world religions are represented in this area: Buddhism, Hinduism, Islam, and Christianity. Linguistic diversity among the groups is also significant; there are more than ten different languages spoken alongside Bengali and Chittagonian.[1] The hill people were generally described by visitors to the region as belonging to the Mongolian group (e.g. Mills, 1935, p. 7), more closely resembling people of Northeast India and Myanmar than the Bengali population in Bangladesh.

The largest group in the CHT is the Muslim Bangladeshi population, who do not engage in swidden cultivation but work in trade and commerce, mostly in the towns. The second largest group is the Chakma group, who have integrated with Bangladeshi culture linguistically and by wearing Bangladeshi-style clothes, albeit with tribal fabrics. The third largest group, and the focus of this book, is the Marma community.

For the next section, see the historical timeline in Appendix B.

The history of the CHT

> The hills and sea-board of Chittagong, until the rise and consolidation of British power, were formerly the battle-ground upon which several races struggled for supremacy. Indigenous hill-tribes, Burmese, Portuguese, and Mahomedans, all preceded us as masters of the country, and each had left behind traces of their rule.
>
> (Lewin, 1885, p. 124)

The earliest historical descriptions of the CHT were written by British government officials. Francis Buchanan[2] in 1798, Thomas H. Lewin[3] from 1839 to 1916, Robert Henry Sneyd Hutchinson[4] in 1906, and John P. Mills from 1926 to 1927[5] – all wrote reports that focused on the large ethnic groups of Chakma, Marma, and Tripura. German ethnographers Emil Riebeck and Adolf Bastian[6] travelled in the region and published their insights from a trip made in 1882. Before his seminal work *The Elementary Structures of Kinship* (1969), Claude Lévi-Strauss wrote in 1952 the little-known work *Kinship Systems of Three Chittagong Hill Tribes*, in which he describes the kinship of the "Mogh" people, later to be known as the Marma. Between 1951 and 1960, the French anthropologist Lucien Bernot and his wife Denise studied language in the area and produced monographs on the Marmas and Sak (more widely known as *Chak*). The Dutch historian, anthropologist, and sociologist Willem van Schendel studied the borderlands of CHT from the 1990s until today, mapping the historical identities of all the CHT ethnic groups as they experienced political change in the region. And more recently, Bangladeshi scholars Abdul Khan and D. M. Barua have contributed research on the topics of Buddhism (Khan, 1999a; Khan 1999b; Barua, 2019), M. Ashrafuzzaman on land rights of indigenous people (Ashrafuzzaman, 2014), B. P. Barua on national integration (Barua, 2001), and Nasir Uddin on the politics of cultural difference (Uddin, 2010), to name but a few of the many local scholars.

The CHT has therefore been a subject of study for British colonial government representatives, explorers, and adventurers, including prominent anthropologists and sociologists, mainly from France, Germany and the Netherlands, and recently local Bangladeshi scholars.

The three powers: the Arakan, the Mughals, and the British

From the literature on the CHT area we learn that during the sixteenth century Chittagong was the base for Portuguese merchants, who engaged in slave trading with the Burmese Arakan kingdoms,[7] trading captives from the indigenous populations of the area. From the 1600s, the kings of Arakan intermittently ruled over the district of Chittagong. The region then became part of the Mughal Empire in the period up to 1750 and the hill chiefs of Chittagong paid a trade tribute or tax to the Mughals. In 1760, the East India Company[8] gained a foothold on the subcontinent mainly by trading cotton, silk, indigo dye, saltpetre, tea, and opium. The commercial enterprise morphed into military and administrative power that took control in 1787 of the whole CHT region, forcing its leaders to pay tax to the company. There were still two prominent leaders in the CHT by the late eighteenth century: the Chakma *Raja* in the central and northern hill tracts, and the Bohmong *Raja* in the south.

East India Company rule in the region lasted until 1858, when the British Crown assumed direct administration of India.

The Asian borderlands and the CHT were on the fringes of British India. However, the skirmishes and unrest in the CHT eventually led to the British Empire taking over the administration of the CHT region to prevent "raids" from the Lushai peoples (Hutchinson, 1906, pp. 8–13). Significantly, in 1860, the CHT region was annexed and became part of the province of Bengal but retained its separate status under the control of an officer with the title of Superintendent of the Hill Tribes.[9] In 1860 the hill tracts were also divided into three administrative circles: the Chakma Circle in the central region of Rangamati; the Bohmong Circle, covering the south and north-west of CHT; and the Mong Circle in Khagrachari district in the north. See Figure 1 for a map of the CHT and Figure 2 for symbols from each royal circle. Moreover,

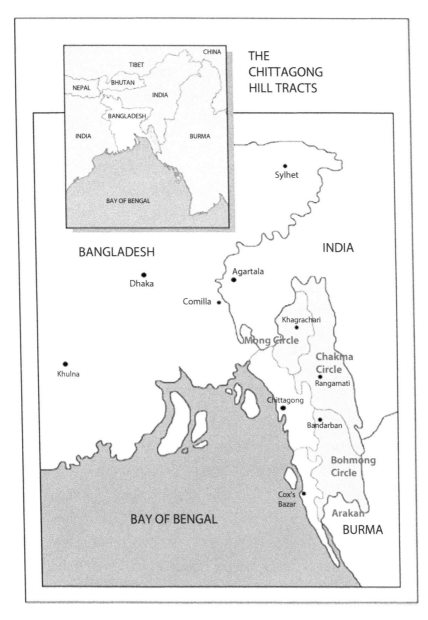

Figure 1 Map of CHT (Roy, 2000, p. 20).

the residents of the three circles were seen not as British subjects but as tributaries.

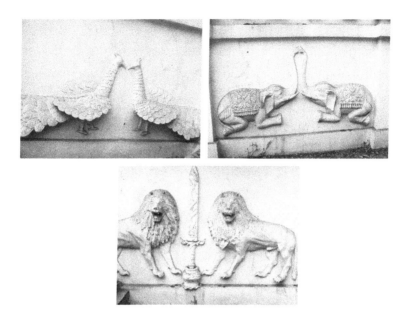

Figure 2 The Mong Circle represented by the symbol of the peacock, the Chakma Circle by the elephant, and the Bohmong Circle by the lion and sword.

In the 1860s, the CHT became an excluded zone that officially separated the CHT region from the plains. This was not just topographical but a cultural separation also. The Bengalis lived in the plains and the non-Bengalis in the hills.

The most important law to govern the region came with the CHT Regulations Act of 1900, also often referred to as the CHT manual. The 1900 Regulations Act took the existing system of chiefs and streamlined and simplified it as part of British efforts to invent a hierarchy of power. The Act provided for the investiture of the chiefs and the appointment of the headmen, as well as stipulating the manner and extent of the local customary laws of the ethnic groups. Each circle chief was made responsible for the collection of revenues and vested with the power to look after internal affairs such as land disputes and other social matters that emerged out of the circles. These circles were further divided into *mouzas* – clusters of villages with a territorial boundary. Each *mouza* fell under the control of a headman, and every village within the *mouza* was represented by a *karbari* (the village head). The internal matters of each village community were decided by its members, including a council of elders under the leadership of the *karbaris*. The 1900 Regulations Act turned the diverse ethnic groups into a single system of chiefs–headmen–village leaders and resulted in a more efficient engine for the collection of *jhum* tax revenue.

The three circles of power, with a hill chief in each circle, made indirect rule of the region by outsiders possible. It also placed negotiating partners in the hill tracts, who were then held responsible for any trouble that emerged from the region. James Scott (2009) describes this process of indirect rule, initiated by colonial powers and then continued by new State power, as a "hill-chief fetish".

> The state's desire for chiefs and the ambitions of upland local strongmen coincided often enough to create imitative state-making in the hills... Local chiefs had ample reason to seek the seals, regalia, and titles conferred by a more powerful realm... Recognition of a lowland realm's imperial charisma was, at the same time, entirely compatible with remaining outside its administrative reach and with a disdain for the subject populations of these lowland realms.
>
> (Scott, 2009, p. 114)

This period came to be remembered as the golden age for the ethnic groups of the hills: even though the British Empire benefitted hugely from tax revenue, the local circles enjoyed their support and protection while ruling their own people with relative autonomy (Ahamed, 2004, p. 236). Moreover, the CHT in its separateness came to enjoy legal protection of its distinct culture and land rights.

However, the situation changed drastically after India's independence from the British Empire in 1947.

Partition of India and the Pakistan phase (1947–1971)

In August 1947, the Indian subcontinent won independence from 300 years of British rule. It was divided into two independent nation states: a Hindu-majority India and a Muslim-majority Pakistan. Immediately, this triggered one of the greatest migrations in human history as millions of Muslims left their homes behind to journey to either West or East Pakistan (later to become Bangladesh), while millions of Hindus and Sikhs moved in the opposite direction to India.

As an excluded area, the CHT did not fall under the jurisdiction of the Bengal Boundary Commission headed by Sir Cyril Radcliffe. Because of this exclusion, the hill people were not represented in the Bengal Legislative Assembly and thus had no voice in the deliberations of 20 June 1947, which debated the questions around the partition of the region. Namely, to which nation the CHT should be assigned. Pakistan had received a poorer share in the partition of Punjab and did not gain Calcutta, which was given to West Bengal and India. Radcliffe tried to compensate Pakistan by including the Chittagong region as part of East Pakistan. The CHT was to be treated as the hinterland of the port city of Chittagong – the only major port remaining in East Bengal after Calcutta. Thus, the CHT was awarded to Pakistan even though it did not have a Muslim majority at the time. Moreover, the verdict of the Commission ignored the right to self-determination of the tribes of the CHT, who preferred to stay within India.

New policies were adopted by the Pakistani regime in the name of "national development" and "national integration". The most significant government-sponsored project was the 1960 Kaptai Hydroelectric Project on the Karnafuli River.[10] From then on, the region experienced commercialisation on a huge scale with the building of the Karnafuli Paper Mill, which made full use of forest reserves to secure pulpwood for making paper. The result of these development projects was catastrophic for local hill tribes, as the Kaptai project saw more than 40 per cent of the best cultivable land submerged under the reservoir of the Kaptai Dam. The displacement of approximately 100,000 hill peoples – mostly Chakma – resulted in them becoming environmental refugees overnight, spilling over into other areas of the CHT and migrating to India (Sopher, 1963, pp. 337–362). Thus, the hill tribes entered this new phase of history with the loss of land, displacement, distrust, and conflict.

The first major changes to the CHT manual were also made during Pakistani rule in 1964, when Pakistan took away the special status of the CHT as an "excluded area", redefining it instead as a "tribal area" within the scope of the legislature of East Pakistan (Adnan, 2008, p. 45). As a result, the CHT was no longer officially designated as a separate homeland for the "indigenous people".

Instead, under amendments to Rule 34 of the 1900 Regulations, the Deputy Commissioner was empowered to distribute hilly lands to the family of hill or "non-hill men" residents.[11] This significant change resulted in the transplanting of land-hungry valley populations to the hills as part of a strategy of "engulfment" (Scott, 2009, p. xii).[12] The amendment to the CHT manual therefore made it possible to facilitate Bengali in-migration to the CHT. This process of legal and commercial "Bengalisation" of the hills was perceived by the hill peoples as an invasion of their homelands.[13] The next phase further incorporated the CHT into the nation state by demanding the ethnic and cultural integration of the CHT with Bangladesh.

Bangladesh as an independent state (1971–)

The Pakistani period of rule came to an end after the Bangladesh War of Independence. The war ended on 16 December 1971, with the help of Indian forces, as East Pakistan won independence from West Pakistan and the new nation came to be known as Bangladesh. This violent end to West Pakistan's rule and the emergence of a new state in the region also had an impact on the CHT. Soon after the Pakistani Army withdrew from the CHT, the *Mukti Bahini* (liberation forces of Bangladesh) went on a rampage against the hill people, accusing them of working against the Bangladesh liberation war. The Chakma *Raja* had aligned himself with Pakistan and was treated as a war collaborator, while the other *Rajas* escaped punishment since they had remained neutral.

Immediately after the conflict with Pakistan, the leader of the newly independent Bangladesh, Sheikh Mujibur Rahman,[14] insisted that the ethnic groups of the hill tracts should integrate and adopt Bengali identity.

> Assimilation to Bengali culture and the transformation into Bengalis, which was proposed by the Sheikh, was regarded as a way to overcome backwardness and adapt to more modern lifestyles.
>
> (Visser and Gerharz, 2016, p. 370)

Throughout the history of the region and especially after 1970, the settlement of Bengali peasants in the hills became part of a "civilising process" that aimed to contribute to the cultural development of the hill tribes. However, the Kaptai project had undermined the CHT's *jhum* economy, and by opening the doors to Bengali in-migration, the developments combined to create an atmosphere of distrust in the CHT. A history of passive resistance against the state in the CHT gave way to open rebellion and Bangladeshi armed forces moved in as full-scale guerrilla warfare ensued. New migrants were brought in under army protection and given arms. By 1990, a continuous war had produced thousands of casualties and led to an exodus of over 70,000 hill people to refugee camps in Tripura state (India) (Van Schendel, 1992, p. 83).

Over time, the people of the Chittagong hills had to come to terms with administrative institutions that had been developed in Bengal: they had to learn the Bengali language to communicate with agents of the state, and local cultures developed a relationship with Bengali culture which was ambiguous. Efforts to adapt to and participate in Bengali culture were counterbalanced by assertions of the worth of each local culture. In 1973, a guerrilla tribal army – *Santi Bahini* – was created, and with backing from the Indian Government launched continual attacks on Bengali settlers in the CHT. To protect the settlers, the Bangladesh police and the military established an increasing presence in the CHT region.[15]

A Peace Accord was signed between the Bangladesh government and the Parabatya Chattagram Jana Samhati Samiti (United People's Party of the Chittagong Hill Tracts) in 1997, and the larger hill groups were invited to take part in national power.

Contemporary times

Common to all three circle chiefs is that they have historically collected tax for the external powers in the region and this practice continues to this day. While the circle chief position may be transferred to another family, the kingly duties and the knowledge therein can become diluted over time. The headmen therefore have the role of being permanent upholders of the rules and norms of the circles. The headmen are knowledge centres that have upheld the 1900 Act and hill tribe traditions through their duties as magistrates and their interpretation of customary law. In this respect they are similar to civil servants, maintaining a "status quo" and handing down knowledge and wisdoms to support the circle structure as new kings from different families assume power. Once appointed, their role and authority are handed down from father to son.

The three circles have reacted differently to the organisation of their group from the outside. When the period of the excluded area came to an end, the CHT region saw an in-migration of

Bengalis which forced the communities to accommodate and assimilate with Bengali culture or resist.

The Chakma Circle

The Chakma king of the early 1960s – *Raja* Tridiv Roy – had aligned himself more closely to the representatives of the Pakistan state and then with West Pakistan in the War of Independence. With the defeat of West Pakistan, he chose to relinquish his power as circle chief to go into exile in Pakistan. In contrast, his son Devashish Roy works with the Bangladeshi state, taking on roles as state minister and other positions. At the same time, the Chakma *Raja* is an advocate for the rights of the hill communities in the CHT as member of the United Nations Permanent Forum on Indigenous Issues. After the Peace Accord, it appears that the Chakma community as a whole was more culturally assimilated to state culture than other hill tribes.

The Mong Circle

The Mong circle is the poorest of the circles but also borders with the insurgency-rife Siliguri Corridor of Northeast India. The Mong Circle has experienced more civil war, upheaval, and violence than all the other circles and consequently has experienced an entrenchment of the Bangladeshi military in the region.

The Bohmong Circle

What is interesting to note from this chapter is that, while all three circles have experienced the same involvement from the outside, it is the Marma circle that appears to be relatively unchanged while the other circles have been assimilating to varying degrees to Bengali culture.

The Bohmong Circle is known as being the most safe and peaceful circle. Some respondents attribute this to the huge number of temples and relics in Bandarban district, which is thought to have spiritually protected the Marma people from both internal strife and external interference.

Key takeaways

The plotted history of the CHT has revealed that the rulers – from the Mughals to the British Empire, from West Pakistan to the new State of Bangladesh – and their different types of rule were the major social forces that shaped the region.

Through the CHT manual, which is still in operation today, the British achieved a centralisation of power and the integration of the diverse ethnic groups into three administrative systems. As a result, the CHT region had experienced autonomy from the rest of the Indian subcontinent. The communities were able to co-exist peacefully together and evolve in isolation, far away from the influence of the state while being subject to tax collection from the British. The CHT appears to have remained stable until the first insurgencies surfaced in the 1970s. The main reason for the stability was due to the administrative structures of the three circles, which reinforced the structures that already existed. Moreover, placing the *Raja* on top of a pyramid structure of power was important for British tax collection purposes, and the annual tax collection ceremony affirmed this hierarchical organisation, albeit the ceremony is being commemorated only in the Bohmong Circle to this day.

Now the CHT region is undergoing even more change. While British influence promoted stability in order to extract tax revenues from the CHT, there has been a shift of power from the traditional circle chiefs to the state after the Peace Accord. This has resulted in the state being more involved in the administration of the region. There is also a lack of representation of the Hill communities in national politics, with the exception of the Chakma people. Furthermore, the CHT manual was initially set up to protect the rights of the hill communities. However, this was amended at the time of the region's loss of autonomy, and the in-migration of the landless refugees from the plains, all of which has changed the landscape and demographics of the CHT region.

3
A toolkit to study identity on the borderlands

A brief summary

Studying the identity of groups in complex and fluid borderlands can be a daunting prospect! The purpose of this chapter is to outline in broad strokes the argument for the role of anthropology in understanding the lived experience of communities on the borderlands. Here are some of the theories from sociology and anthropology that provide insights into studying ethnic identities in fluid regions of the world. By using not one but different theoretical lenses, I will demonstrate how to understand the many processes behind the creation and maintenance of a unique identity such as that of the Marma. This chapter is a summary of the full chapter, which can be found in Appendix C.

Understanding borderlands

Ethnic groups that live in the CHT can negotiate life in the shatter zones in different ways: they can assimilate to dominant state culture, temporarily align and speak as one group, or strongly differentiate themselves from other ethnic groups through, for example, language, history, and material objects.

When ethnic groups assimilate

The Marma people have maintained core cultural practices in the fluid borderlands. The group's practices seem to run contrary to the choices made by their neighbours in the CHT, who have slowly assimilated to the culture of the nation state.

Here's an example of what might be called the "typical" response to assimilation. The Chakma people, displaced by a loss of their Chakma lands, are an example of continual adaption and assimilation to state power in the region. Recently, a clause in the CHT Peace Accord supported a quota system for "tribals" in government services and educational institutions. This resulted in the migration of Chakma students and their immersion in the culture of Dhaka and other major urban centres. Moreover, the Chakma lower classes made up around 70 per cent of the migrants who worked in the garment industry on the outskirts of the major cities in Bangladesh (Visser and Gerharz, 2016, pp. 370–376).

While some borderland groups assimilate, others respond to inter-ethnic contact and interdependence by accentuating their distinctness.

Creating cultural boundaries

In *Ethnic Groups and Boundaries* (1969), Frederik Barth posited that when cultures come into contact with other cultures, boundaries tend to be drawn around selected characteristics of the group. This selection process creates separation, which in turn helps to define the group for themselves and for others. A group maintains its identity by determining criteria for membership and ways of signalling membership and exclusion on the boundaries of culture. In effect, Barth sees distinct identities and traditions arising out of contact with and opposition to others, and not only because of isolation.

Hybridity: multicultural unities

Moving away from theories that tackle differentiation on the boundaries of culture, this section will shift the focus away from the processes on the boundaries of culture to the processes that create the content of culture from within groups.

When more than one ethnic group rub alongside each other, they can join together around an emblematic ethnic value to form a hybrid group. These same societies can see themselves as unified while at the same time being plural or having multicultural unities within the unity. The concepts of creolisation, entanglement, and hybridity describe another aspect of plurality, where there is an integration of subgroups into one group. There is a fusion of different languages and the amalgamation of elements from different cultures to create one society. Moreover, the concepts provide insights into how groups are constantly changing from within to respond to the needs of the external environment, differentiating the overall group on the Barthian boundaries of culture.

Creolisation

The idea of creolisation originates from linguistic theory in which a new language such as Yiddish or Creole is created from two different languages.

Entanglement

In *Entangled Objects*, Thomas (1991) argues that "entangled objects", which are foreign artefacts of material culture, have been appropriated by indigenous people and incorporated within a framework of local meanings. Therefore, "cultures" construct ethnicity when they comes into contact or tension with outsiders. He further argues that, internally, beneath the level of ethnicity, societies are cosmopolitan spaces of entanglement.

Syncretism

During migration, ethnic groups will either carry over or discard cultural elements of the group as they reach their new home. This process is called "syncretism".

Models of chaos

Michael Scott's (2005) concept of chaos in locality posits that the separation from all that is familiar, to settle in new lands, stimulates the integration of the subgroups into one unified entity. Another of Scott's case studies on cultural hybridity describes the chaos that comes with blocked bodies. Scott refers to the violence of the 1972 massacres of Hutu by Tutsi in Burundi. The practice of dismemberment was, in his view, a response to the blending of identities between Hutu and Tutsi to the point that it was no longer possible to distinguish between the two identities.

A recap

To conclude, each theorist treats hybridity differently. Theories of creolisation, entanglement, syncretism, and the model of chaos reveal the processes involved in the integration of subgroups into one group while differentiating the overall group on the Barthian boundaries of culture. The theories provide insights into how groups are constantly changing from within the group according to the needs of the external environment. All of the processes described by the authors in this section have relevance to the Marma cultural and ethnic trends and the book will draw upon some of these approaches pragmatically at different junctures in the study.

The invention of tradition and culture

This section covers explanations on how the structures of some communities are able to appear unchanging over time – both externally and to their inhabitants.

Invention of tradition

Where a strong ethnic identity exists, a group's culture often appears to be rooted in traditions that are handed down and considered sacred and binding, and therefore are both unchanged and unchangeable. However, historical analysis usually shows that, while some content has been transmitted over long periods, traditional forms are often invented rather than received, and re-invented in accordance with contemporaneous needs, circumstances, and creative urges.

Invention of culture

Ongoing cultural representations refer to or take account of prior representations, and in this sense the present has continuity with the past. It encompasses both continuity and discontinuity – with the balance in favour of discontinuity – in the attribution of new meaning in the present through reference to the unchanging past.

Inversion of tradition

Thomas (1992) claims that difference is created through contact with the other, not only at the level of boundary-making but also within culture itself and that culture can be further inverted in response to impositions by, for example, the colonising other.

A recap

These perspectives on invented traditions and culture demonstrate how encounters with forces outside a community can push societies to differentiate themselves through inventions or inversions that can be continuously or periodically reinvented. From these vantage points, we can see how customs and traditions can change over time as conventions are adjusted to meet new needs, all the while maintaining an essential core.

The reproduction and transformation of culture

To better understand how the core of a group's tradition, culture, and identity is reproduced in ways that maintain boundaries and set the group apart in spite of hybridisations and inventions, it is necessary to consider an alternative grouping of anthropological literature. In its premise and focus, the literature in the next section shifts the balance away from discontinuity within tradition to continuity within change. In this way, it may be possible to understand how core processes are able to endure in contexts of change and instability.

Here we will look at anthropological approaches that focus on the role of structures in the reproduction of culture and the various ways agency can work within stable structures to enact change over time.

Structure in reproduction and transformation

There are theories that combine both structure with agency in its different forms to show how structure can be reproduced over time and transformed.

Structure in the historical *longue durée*

Fernand Braudel studied the relationship between agency and environment over the *longue durée*.[1] Braudel saw that the *longue durée* was not eternal but had a beginning and an end, and by viewing societies in this way, it would be possible to see what happened to structures over time. He also noted that structures that could not be adapted would eventually cease to exist.

The book includes theorists who demonstrate the importance of studying structures over time to see how they are reproduced. Leach's Kachins were the same at the beginning and at the end of the historical timeline with some structural variation achieved. Sahlin's islanders work within their cultural schemas to incorporate encounters with "the other", and through a process of appropriation over their historical *longue durée* they are slowly transformed as a society. In contrast, Ortner's Sherpa actors respond to and work with the structural contradictions in their inheritance rules to move to better positions within society and, in the process, instigate the transformation in values of the celibate Buddhist monastery.

In this book, we will explore Marma agency on structures, whether on marriage rules or when material culture helps the group to reproduce structures and maintain continuity within contexts of change. This kind of agency is limited to adapting and absorbing, to perpetuating and reproducing structures and the overall system.

Employing the various ideas and approaches of this chapter, the next chapters will now explore the ways in which this seemingly stable society is busy accentuating its difference to other groups in a fast-changing environment on the borderlands.

4
Marma kinship and marriage rituals

> Kinship and marriage are about the basic facts of life. They are about "birth, and copulation, and death", the eternal round that seemed to depress the poet, but which excites, among others, the anthropologist.
>
> (Fox, 1967, p. 27)

One of the markers of group identity is in its kinship rules and customs. Marma's kinship structures and practices have set the stage for, and contributed to, their distinct identity formation and have been intentionally adapted to respond to the changing demographics of the CHT.

To demonstrate this uniqueness, this chapter will compare other kinship systems – from the plains of Bangladesh to the hill tracts – with the kinship rules practised by the Marma. These other kinship systems could have exerted pressure on the Marma to adopt, for example, the same marriage practices. However, the temptation has been rejected in favour of retaining a "traditional" system of Marma kinship and marriage customs that have endured, according to literature sources, since the 1800s if not earlier.

This chapter will study the relational underpinnings of Marma ethnicity: how the Marma people invest in a system of kinship and marriage that make up the key elements of Marma uniqueness and ethnic persistence. The main focus will be on the extent to which the Marma people practise clan exogamy, which is the custom of marrying outside a family clan but within the ethnic group, as opposed to clan endogamy, which is the custom of marrying within the limits of an ethnic group only (more on this in the next chapter).

The chapter will conclude with an in-depth piece of ethnography on Marma marriage rituals and a discussion around the whole process of marriage. It will illustrate how Marma marriage rules and rituals are part of a culturally rooted tradition that is fully lived and experienced on the borderlands.

Kinship practices in the region

The principles of social cohesion are formally ordered by kinship, lineage, and genealogy. Studying kinship in this corner of the world, however, is challenging given that it is a meeting point between different ethnicities and religions with various histories of migration and assimilation. This section will describe a selection of different kinship systems and their unique characteristics as a backdrop to the study of Marma kinship.

Chakma kinship

The largest tribal group in the CHT – the Chakma – were studied by Lévi-Strauss (1952a) and more recently by Barua (2001). Lévi-Strauss notes that Chakma kinship terms are the only ones in the CHT that are mostly derived from Bengali. According to

Barua, kinship groups of Chakma society are called *goza*, and are divided into numerous *gusti* or patriclans. The Chakma can marry both within the *goza* (endogamous) or outside the *goza* (exogamous). The Chakma follow patrilineal descent, and inheritance is transmitted from father to sons (Barua, 2001, pp. 36–37). From Lévi-Strauss, we learn that both parallel marriage with a mother's sister's daughter and cross-cousin marriage with a father's sister's daughter and mother's brother's daughter can take place. Moreover, there are two routes to marriage. Firstly, there is marriage by elopement. When the guilty couple are tracked down and caught, they have to pay a fine of money and a pig. Should the couple elope a further three times, the marriage becomes final and the girl's parents have to accept their daughter's choice. Secondly, there is marriage by purchase. In this case, the bridegroom's family raise a bride price that includes money, ornaments, cloth, pigs, rice, and rice beer. Marriage is ordinarily patrilocal except when the father is close to his daughter – then the couple also have the option to live with the girl's family (Lévi-Strauss, 1952a, pp. 42–43).

Bangladeshi kinship

Since rural Bangladesh is similar to the hill tracts, Mashreque's 1998 study of kinship in rural Bangladesh provides comparative insights into Bangladeshi kinship. We learn that the descent principle is patrilineal with patrilocal residence, with the shift of residence usually undertaken by the bride. Members of the patrilineage and extended patrilocal families live in a common residential compound called homestead or *bari* containing several small houses. The internal cohesion of the kinship structure remains the function of the *bari* head and patrilineage is the core of the social organisation incorporating all the agnates and their spouses. The *bari* head arbitrates small disputes in the courtyard between the interacting households and arrangement of family events and rituals like birth, circumcision, and marriage is usually made in consultation with the *bari* head (Mashreque, 1998, p. 52).[1] However, bilateral descent principles also operate, as the maternal kinship connection is often valued. However, the degree of matrilineality is not significant in rural Bengali groups compared to the Chakma kinship, and as we will see, in the Marma system.

Shenk (2016) examines consanguineous marriage patterns in rural Bangladesh, where the traditionally agrarian region is increasingly engaging with the global market economy, and the challenges this places on marriage preferences. A consanguineous marriage is a union between two individuals who are related as second cousins or closer. Marriages are generally arranged by parents, with a focus on endogamy within families. The advantages of these marriage unions are that they reinforce existing kin relatedness, cohesiveness, and loyalty to one's kin group. Importantly, consanguineous marriages allow kin groups to keep dowries small and limit the subdivision of property and/or the sharing of such property with non-kin.[2] Poorer households are more likely to engage in consanguineous unions because of their inability to pay a dowry up front, while wealthier parents who are able to pay higher dowries are motivated to search for a husband outside of the kin group.[3] Therefore, both endogamy and exogamy marriage practices are in operation in Bangladeshi kinship (Shenk et al., 2016, pp. 169–177). The patrilineal descent principles regulate the possession of ancestral property and they follow the Muslim law of inheritance, with the son being entitled to two-thirds share of his father's property and a daughter to one-third share. Although a Muslim woman is legally entitled to inherit a small portion of ancestral property, she is expected to give up the claim in favour of her brothers. In exchange, she receives gifts and valuable possessions and can expect protection from her natal family (Mashreque, 1998, pp. 56–57).

Marma principles of descent, rules, and residence

Patriclans

Marma kinship is a mix of various settlement patterns that reflect the wave of migrations into the area across four centuries of Marma history. My observations in the field corroborate the earlier works of Lévi-Strauss (1952a and 1952b) and Bernot (1967), in that the Marma group are divided into patrilineal descent groups and each group lives in and are defined by their particular locality. These descent groups migrated separately but at some point converged in the CHT to establish the Marma community. More details on this will be covered in the chapter on Marma migration and settlement, but for the purposes of understanding Marma kinship, this section will briefly cover the most salient points that relate to kinship.

The earliest descriptions of CHT clans come from Lewin (1885) when he describes the dwellers of the hill tracts roughly as two clans: Khyoung-tha, or children of the river, and Toung-tha, children of the hill. In the late 1800s, the Khyoung-tha were made up of one group of 36,000 "Mughs" under the Bohmong; they lived near the river, were of Arakanese descent, followed Buddhism, and spoke the language "of which Burmese is a modern offshoot" (Lewin, 1885, p. 226). Lewin sees the Toung-tha as being of Singpho origin but also made up of different groups of different origins.[4]

The Marma group came to be defined by the locations of their settlement as they collectively worked on establishing the new boundaries of their land. The Bohmong was not seen as a traditional clan chief but a leader in exile from Burma that led a hybrid group during its migration across the region. The Marma clans practise clan exogamy since clan members consider themselves to be of common blood and therefore marriage with one's own clan would be like a marriage with one's own family and therefore taboo. Thus clan exogamy and, as we will see later in this book, tribal endogamy go hand in hand in the Marma community.

Residence: the compound or *oeingsa*

Lévi-Strauss noted that the Mog clans were patrilineal but with some matrilineal elements in the household (Lévi-Strauss, 1952a, pp. 211–212). Defining the "household" from a Marma perspective, a Marma household is called an *oeingsa* with branch households established within the vicinity of the main or core household, sometimes even as part of the main household. Like the Bangladesh *bari*, the Marma compound is made up of patrilineal family units headed by the eldest brother of the family.

In my host family (see Figure 3), the eldest brother of the family lived in the centre of the compound and all his siblings lived

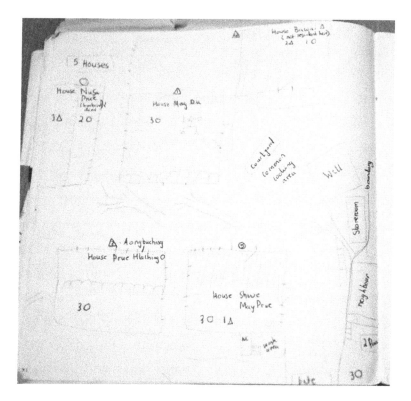

Figure 3 The host family compound of five households. Diagram shows layout of compound as well as family composition. The triangle represents male and circle, female. This image was created with help from family members and captured in my ethnographic journal.

around him. In the main household of the senior brother, the eldest daughter was unmarried, the second had eloped with a Bengali Hindu, and the third had married my local helper in the town – Shai Shing Aung. In the compound, another brother had married a Rakine from Cox's Bazar and the family were dress makers. One of the brothers had died and had left a widow and her children. The only sister – Shwe May Prue of the main household – lived with her husband, and two of her daughters at the time of fieldwork were married and resided abroad.[5] One daughter was at home and another son eventually went abroad. The family of the sister – Shwe May Prue – were the wealthiest of all the families on the compound, but still daily respect was shown to the eldest brother. During my visit, I came to learn that all members of this compound shared in shopping, food preparations, and religious rituals, and went on organised trips to various local temples.[6]

From the host family in Bandarban town, we can see the distinctive features of Marma *oeingsa* organisation that strengthen the family as it links members by economic, social, and ritual cooperation. This household organisation is a common feature of both the royal and non-royal families, and in both rural and urban settings (Ahamed, 2004, pp. 120–123; Khan, 1999a, pp. 61–63). Additionally, Ahamed details the extent of the cooperation in the rural setting of Roangchari, placing food sharing as central to the relationship:

> [T]he way *oeingsa* is defined among the Marma people has various crosscutting aspects between kin and non-kin, between sharing or not sharing food. Marma often say even distant members of the lineage can be included as members of *oeingsa* as long as they eat from the same cooking pot and share economic activities.
>
> (Ahamed, 2004, p. 121)

The *oeingsa* is therefore not only a biological unit but also a unit of economic cooperation. However, in the urban setting, only those with access to land, property, and some wealth can maintain an *oeingsa* compound and therefore a system of social and economic cooperation.

The freedom of Marma women

One important characteristic that differentiates the Marma people from the Chakma and Bangladeshi populations are that women enjoy more freedom in a selection of a husband. When Lewin (1885) writes about the custom of marriage by elopement, he is effectively saying that a couple can force a marriage to take place and that the bride-to-be has agency in making this happen. The young men of the village go in pursuit of the runaway couple. If they are caught, the girl is asked if she wants to leave her family home, and if she agrees, then the lover is fined by the girl's family. If the lover cannot pay or come to a new arrangement, he is beaten by the community (Lewin, 1885, p. 232).

Lévi-Strauss also observed in the 1950s that women have more freedom:

> On a more psychological level, one is struck by the great freedom enjoyed by women, contrasting with both the Hindu and the Muslim patterns which have permeated Cakma society to a greater extent.
>
> (Lévi-Strauss, 1952a, p. 51)

To this day, elopement remains the strategy to force a marriage in the Marma community. During the fieldwork, I came to learn that Dolly and her husband had known each other all their lives and were expected to marry. Dolly's partner was eager to leave the area to work but wanted to take Dolly with him. However, he was not in a financial position to offer a huge bride price. They forced the issue by eloping to the nearest town on the coast – Cox's Bazar. The parents were outraged, and in order to regain the honour for their daughter they organised a hasty wedding and the bride price was put on hold until Dolly's partner could raise the funds. Dolly and her partner could share from the same plate at the wedding and the holding of hands was witnessed by the community. This route saved on family expenses because the wedding had to be organised with haste. However, elopement can be a source of shame in that it exposes the fact that the child has not shown courtesy to his or her parents as filial respect is important. If elopement is the result of parents' disapproval, there is an even greater loss of face. Moreover, there is a blemish on the daughter as it is assumed that she has already had sexual relations with her partner.

> Hence, elopement, in a typical Burmese circumlocution, is compared to the exchange of an unripe jackfruit, which has been beaten to look ripe, for a copper coin, which has been polished with mercury to look like silver.
>
> (Spiro, 1977, p. 191)

Since the Marma group are mainly patrilocal, the bride usually follows the husband to his family home: the *Khamaji* (bride) *Laikte* (following husband). These customs and practices are broadly in line with Bangladeshi marriage customs. However, some of the characteristics related to a Marma marriage (and inheritance) rules are more complex and ambiguous. Unlike other patrilineal groups within and outside of the CHT, such as the Bawm, Tanchangya, and Bangladeshi, the Marma people are exceptional in allowing Marma women to enjoy a substantial degree of authority in terms of a share of the inheritance of property and decision-making in the household. The Marma group also accept a daughter's husband as a member of the household if the husband is not able to offer patrilocal residence. This was the case for princess Lily's household. Her father was a non-royal who lived in the royal compound with his princess wife.

Moreover, if a Marma couple have only one daughter, the patrilineal descent rule of the Marma people is subordinated to a form of "matrilocality" where the daughter's husband moves to the residence of his in-laws.[7] Matrilocal residence – *Thamak* (son-in-law) *takt* (lives in house with her) – often comes with no social stigma attached to the male, even though in Bangladeshi society this would be considered a lowering of the social status of the husband. The Marma group, therefore, follow both patrilocal and matrilocal residence patterns. Significantly, if a husband in a matrilocal setting inherits property or land from his own family, the husband will take this with him to his new home. If he dies, his wife becomes the caretaker of his inherited land until his heirs come of age.

Summary

A comparative look at communities in and around the CHT on ideal marriage and residence rules reveals the specificity of Marma kinship. In Table 1, the summary of the key features of regional kinship practices show that the elements that make Marma rules unique revolve around the position of women in Marma society. Marma girls can choose who they marry. There is provision for an inheritance for women (to be covered in Chapter 5), as well as the possibility of matrilocal residence. It seems that the Marma people have more in common with Chakma on marriage customs with the bridegroom's family giving wealth to the bride's family, and both the Marma and Chakma groups are able to force a marriage to happen through elopement. All groups have less in common with the majority Bengali culture, but the Marma *oeingsa* has a similar social organisation to the Bengali *bari* residence, whereby the eldest son oversees the economic cooperation of the households that make up the compound.

There is continuity amid change and continuity despite change. The Marma people have maintained specific customs such as clan exogamy and patrilineal and matrilocal residence, as well the provision of an inheritance for girls, with the earliest literature indicating it as such (Lévi-Strauss, 1952a). These practices are continuous and unique as they differentiate the group from other groups in the region and the nation state.

Marma marriage rituals: "To be put on the path together"

This section will present an in-depth analysis of the ethnographic data on Marma marriage rituals and ceremonies, which are at the core of Marma kinship. It will examine ethnographic data on the arrangement of Marma marriages, the rules, customs, and rituals related to weddings, as well as the social involvement in Marma marriage, which all come together to try and ensure a longstanding marriage. The ethnography will illustrate structural reproduction at work as the agency of various actors throughout the ceremony ensures that marriage rituals are reproduced over time. The continued investment in a system of kinship and marriage is strongly linked to a sense of the fragility of marriage, and the marriage ceremony addresses this fragility. By employing

Table 1 Showing comparative key characteristics of local kinship and descent principles

Group	Succession	Descent	Residence	Marriage preference	Marriage customs	Taboos	Terminology
Chakma	Father to sons	Patrilineal	Patrilocal	Clan exogamy Parallel cousins	Bride purchase Elopement		Bengali
Bengali	Father to sons	Patrilineal	Patrilocal – *bari*	Consanguineous Kin endogamy	Dowry from wife's family		Bengali/Hindu
Marma	Father to sons + daughters	Patrilineal	Patrilocal – *oeingsa*	Bilateral cross cousin Clan exogamy, ethnic endogamy	Girls can choose Bride price Elopement	Parallel cousins from own lineage	Burmese

all the resources – both Buddhist and non-Buddhist – the Marma people are able to reduce the anxiety of family members who depend on a successful marriage in order to reproduce the next generation.

The analysis will demonstrate the uniqueness of the Marma marriage rituals and how they contribute to the reproduction of a distinct culture.

For a full list of terminology, see the Glossary.

The steps involved in a Marma marriage

Consulting astrologers
The compatibility of names

Before an official engagement, the couple's family consult with a well-respected astrologer[8] to check the compatibility of names that are given at birth. At birth, a baby is taken to the *Kyang* (temple) to be presented to the monk. The monk selects three Marma names based on the sibling position, the appearance and characteristics of the baby, and the day of the week of birth. Since the Marma people believe in the Buddhist doctrine of reincarnation, sometimes a child that comes into this world takes on the form of an ancestor and will accordingly take an aspect of the ancestor's name. Naming often reflects the day of the week that a baby was born and this is called a birth day. The compatibility of these birth days for a couple is important. For example, a person born on Saturday may marry someone born on Tuesday, Thursday, and Wednesday; a person born on Sunday is compatible with someone born on a Tuesday and Friday; one born on Monday is "friendly" with Thursday and Friday; one born on Wednesday is "friendly" with Saturday, Thursday, and Monday; one born on Thursday is "friendly" with Tuesday, Wednesday, and Saturday. Thus, to achieve a good outcome for a marriage and future prosperity, the Marma people share their birth days before becoming engaged as it enables prospective partners to see whether they are astrologically compatible.[9]

Birth charts

The astrologer also consults the birth charts of the candidates, taking into account planetary and stellar influences on the birth charts of the couple before he gives the final verdict on whether the pair are astrologically friendly or favourable to each other.[10] The guardians take the birth charts to the Buddhist monk or another expert astrologer. The monk or astrologer consults the two birth charts and decides on the wedding date and the hour considered lucky for the future couple, in the presence of their guardians. He also takes into account cross-cousin rules and preferences.

"I want the daughter for my son" – the engagement process
The proposal

Marriages are arranged, or partially assisted by the two families in the case of acceptable love marriages between cross-cousins. In the first stage, a proposition of marriage is made: several relatives and friends initiate "diplomatic talks", making trips to the two families and their candidates. The process is called *mya* (wife) *mui* (ask) *jaung* (for) *laarey* (going), or "I want the daughter for my son". The initiative comes from the bridegroom's side. On a fortuitous day, which is usually calculated by an astrologer, the bridegroom's parents with some of their friends and relatives, in a group comprising an odd number of people, take a bottle of rice wine to the legal guardian of the would-be bride. In rural settings, they also take a cockerel, which has been boiled, and one special dish, which is usually wild jungle potatoes cooked with dried fish and wrapped in banana leaves. These items are taken to the bride's house before the cock crows or *IngThang Cho* – when marriage speaks.

The negotiation

The *oingh* or "gift of wine", covered in a scarf, is opened when the bride's side agrees to the visit, and then another bottle of wine is produced, which both sides enjoy but this time with a dried fish dish. First the bride's guardians are asked if they have no objection, and then the would-be bride is asked to express her opinion on the marriage. If there is no objection, the deal is closed, the scarf is folded, and a small feast is arranged with the rice wine and food. Another bottle of wine is produced with the gift of a boiled cockerel from the bridegroom's family. The bride's side provide more wine and one hen. In this marriage negotiation, the wine is symbolic of honour, the cockerel represents prosperity, and the hen is a symbol of fertility.

Interpreting dreams

When talking to the elders, I learnt that another step is sometimes added at this early stage of marriage negotiation. The ritual is called the *Ing Mak* (dreams) *Praing* (tell). This time, no chicken is cooked but a dish of aubergine mixed with dried fish is given to the bride's parents. The parents are asked the next day to recount the dreams of the groom and bridegroom. This stage is called "repeat the dream offering". If the dreams are good, the marriage can go ahead. If the dreams are bad, the wedding is terminated. According to the elders, dreams are like omens or signs that need to be interpreted before the final go ahead is given. The parties can also consult a dream specialist who can interpret the dreams from a Burmese book on dreams – *Ink Mak* (dream) *Thui Thunk* (interpret) *Kyaing* (book). For the Marma people, I was told that a marital union in its earliest stages is considered fragile because it holds the potential for disorder, as new members join a household, whether patrilocal or matrilocal. Therefore, much needs to be divined, cosmically aligned, and foretold in the dream-world by specialists in advance of the ceremony. The emphasis upon checking the stars and people's dreams seems to indicate that the Marma attribute a limited efficacy to the marriage exchanges of food and wine. They must arrange marriages in accordance with cosmic tendencies as well as social rules.

Financial details of the marriage

The phase called *Chameng Than Pwe* or *Mengla Tun Pwe* or "to be put on the path together" (Khan, 1999, p. 156) is the formal sitting down of the two families to negotiate the details of the marriage. The elders call it more simply *Thee Thak* (drinks again) *Haaing Thak* (food again). It is a public event as it always includes either the headman or a village elder and the family of the engaged couple. It is paid for by the boy's family and covers three steps: firstly, the negotiation and announcement of the bride price with *Hnaang*

Rey, which means "I am giving gold as a gift to take you as my wife", in which the amount of gold or comparable precious items is negotiated. The amount given reflects the social status of the groom; the bride price, wedding dress, and ornaments are settled as gifts from the groom. Secondly, the wedding date is set; and thirdly, approval is given for the couple to be seen in public and be alone together.

The pre-wedding rituals

The wedding ceremony is a public announcement of a couple's intention to live together. The traditional wedding months are from November until December and February until June. July is avoided as it is the rainy season, which is also the rainy retreat for Buddhist monks and a difficult period for guests to travel to a wedding.

The Marma people are noted for their beautiful and elaborate wedding ceremonies. Having seen several weddings it is interesting to note that no shortcuts are taken. All the steps seem to be followed sequentially, with the same format and overseen by the *medechar*. The *medechar* is a man who is neither a widower nor a divorcee and who lives with one wife and is an expert in interpreting and enacting Marma marriage rituals.

The eve of the wedding day

On the eve of the wedding, relatives are invited to the groom's house to take part in a *nat* spirit *puja* and general celebration. The worship takes place on a bamboo platform adorned with flowers, bamboo stems, and leaves from the jungle. This *nat* ceremony in the evening includes prayers to ancestors, the house spirit, and the village guardian spirits. A sacrificial offering of a pig (*Gong-u-nai-u*) or chickens (*Chungmale*) is made for the ancestors and guardians of the home and village. The men of the house prepare the sacrifice by boiling the chicken or roasting the pig. The *medechar* is then brought into the ceremony to follow the steps of the ritual offering as the best parts of the animals and other food offerings are put together to make a complete dish. The rest of the food is eaten in the company of family and friends. Thus, all those who could possibly influence the success or failure of a marriage are appeased from the outset of a marriage ceremony – the *nat* spirits, the guardian spirits, and the ancestors of the family.

Wedding day procession

At 9 am on the wedding day, the groom's party – made up of an odd-numbered group – walk towards the bride's house in a procession (see Figure 4). The group consists of the bridegroom's parents and people who have married only once and single boys and girls. No widows or divorcees are allowed to take part, which is indicative of how the Marma see marriage as being especially vulnerable to break-down. The group take a boiled cockerel, a handful of boiled rice, a bottle of rice beer, and rice wine to the bride's family. One man carries suitcases that contain dresses and ornaments for the bride. The groom carries a long *dao* (knife)[11] in his hands. At the bride's house, the articles of clothing and ornaments are presented to the bride's family and the younger sister or female cousin of the bride washes the feet of the groom to welcome him into the house. The group members of the bridegroom's side usually help the bride get ready. The gifts of

Figure 4 Newly-wed couple facing barricades.

food and drink are shared by both sides. The groom walks the bride to the wedding hall, often to the backdrop of live music.

Barricades and the stoning myth

Before entering the marriage hall, the groom is separated from the bride by a bamboo stick or small branches of trees, and an entry fee is demanded. Not unlike barricading practices in rural Burma, failure to pay the entry fee results in the groom being threatened with stones or sticks (Spiro, 1977, p. 158). Spiro claims that this demand for money is part of a stoning myth "*kyou tade*", which is related to a rural Burmese origin myth. This custom originated after destruction of the earth and all its inhabitants by fire, water, and wind, which resulted in four gods without sexual organs coming down to earth. They were unable to return to heaven as they ate rice and roots and developed sexual organs, signifying greed, anger, and lust. The higher gods saw them as engaging in sex and stoned them (Spiro, 1977, p. 185). The barricading ritual therefore seems to have emerged from the idea in the origin myth that couples who are transitioning from one state to another – especially from a lower earthly state to a higher heavenly state – need to be obstructed or stoned if they break free. This ceremonial obstruction happens several times on the wedding day. It signals that the wedding ceremony is a ritual enactment of at least part of the origin myth and so, by implication, each wedding recapitulates the first marriage conducted by the demi-gods. Moreover, the barricading seems to block exogamy and a greater bride price or entry fee is required to overcome it. Given that the bride and groom are regaled with shiny emblems of wedding clothes, it seems that entry into the wedding hall and the ceremony is symbolically constructed as a return to where the higher gods reside, suggesting that marriage ceremonies recapitulate the mythical train of events. It is not clear, without more ethnographic detail, whether the subsequent marriage recapitulates the myth, that is, whether they are marrying as figures of the lower world but protected from divine anger or whether they are able to move to a higher plane in spite of their forthcoming sexual union.

Chameng Than Pwe: "To be put on the path together"
Blessings

The entrance of the wedding venue is decorated with two fresh banana plants on either side of the gate and two ceremonial lucky water pots (*rijang-ow*) are filled with water and mango leaves (see Figure 5). The extent of the decorations shows the affluence of the host family.

When the group arrive at the gate of the wedding venue, water from the ceremonial lucky water pots is sprinkled on the couple to welcome them as purification before they take the transitional state – within the context of the stoning myth – from earthly to heavenly states. Then they are led to the inner room where there is a small bamboo table: the groom sits to the right, the bride sits on the left, and two unmarried girls sit next to the bride. All face the invited guests. Again, the *medechar* takes water from the pot and this is sprinkled over the couple to protect them and to drive away unwanted spirits.

A group of Buddhist monks in odd numbers are formally requested to deliver the five precepts[12] and the incantation of the *Mangala Suttra* to ward off evil. The audience in unison repeat the five precepts and with folded hands – a gesture of veneration – listen to the recitation of the suttras. This part is not considered to be part of the wedding ritual since Buddhist monks never

Figure 5 Ceremonial lucky water pots (*rijang-ow*).

"wed" people. In fact a Marma wedding ceremony recapitulates a stoning myth that is not recognised by Buddhism. Instead, the Buddhist incantation of the *Mangala Suttra* is a way of inviting auspiciousness and prosperity into the newlyweds' lives. The monks dip a bunch of mango or blackberry leaves into a water pot which is wrapped in consecrated thread. After lifting from the pot, the monk sprinkles on the heads of the bride and groom with water droplets – five or seven times. When the religious ceremony is over, food is offered to the monks and arrangements are made for their return to the monastery.

The social contract

The bride and groom prostrate in front of their parents to receive blessings. Parents, in front of the headmen and the audience of guests, show approval of the union by reciting a traditional blessing that bestows health, wealth, and a long marriage to the couple. The parents announce the amount of bride price from bridegroom to bride and sometimes a dowry (bride to groom) is presented so that the community can witness the exchange.

Eating from the same dish

Eating from the same dish is called *Ley Chang Tamey* (Khan, 1999, p. 186) or *La Chung Sa Rey* according to the elders. The hands of husband and wife come together with the food when feeding each other. The *medechar* who oversees the wedding ceremony serves food constantly, so it never runs out, just as the marriage is hoped to never come to an end. The mixing of hands and food is a symbol of commensality and marriage. Any leftovers from this meal are wrapped and offered to the river spirit the next morning.

The chicken beak

The *medechar* then performs a ceremony called *chainga*. This involves pulling apart the beak of the chicken along with the lower forked jawbone. He interprets the forked jawbone to predict the future of the relationship. The right bone represents the man, the left the female. The longer the fork, the longer the relationship will last. If the fork on the right side is longer than the left, it means that the husband will outlive the wife and vice versa. The prediction is then checked with other elders in the room, including the headman or village *karbari* (see Figure 6). Examination of a chicken's tongue bone and acceptance of the prediction by the headman is the final seal of societal approval of the union.

Hand over hand

The *medechar* announces the sacredness of the marriage by putting right hands together – *Ley Tha hit* or *Lou Chani* – over boiled chicken and rice or by the members of the family holding hands over a bowl (see Figure 7). Water is then poured over the hands. The water represents marriage as it is as indivisible as water. If the pitcher is full, it means that more resources will be available to the couple. They are now husband and wife: *Langa* (husband) *May* (wife) *Rey* (become).

The sword, more blessings, the meal, and drinks

The *medechar* then presents a long *dao* or sword with several coils of white thread next to it – each coil being made up of five rounds of cotton threads to represent the five Buddhist precepts. When a guest comes to bless the couple, the couple bow, and

Figure 6 Ceremony called *chainga*.

Figure 7 Putting right hands together – *Ley Tha hit* or *Lou Chani*.

the guests scatter uncooked rice, as with sprinkled water, on the couple's heads, possibly to ward off unwanted spirits. Other rituals such as chanting and throwing unhusked rice away from the front door of the groom's house may be performed for the same purpose, possibly to "beat away the wild spirits which may have accompanied the bride from her own patrilineage" (Tapp, 2003, p. 300).

The *medechar* then takes a coil of thread from the knife and hands it to the guest, who in turn puts the coil around the bridegroom's (right-hand) wrist (see Figure 8). When wearing the coil of thread, the point of the knife is taken very close to the fingertips of the bridegroom's wrist to transfer the thread directly to the wrist. Then the bridegroom takes a coil from the knife and places it on the bride's wrist in a similar manner. The bride receives the coil by bowing herself in front of the bridegroom. By way of a blessing, the *medechar* offers a little glass of "rice wine" (distilled rice) or "beer" (fermented rice) to the guests. Teetotallers can avoid the drink by just touching it with their fingers. The guests then give a present to the couple. This process can last for several hours as the Marma wedding can involve many guests. Guests who are younger than the bride cannot bless the couple.

The guests are finally welcomed to sit down and enjoy a meal with drinks.

After the wedding, the bride stays at the groom's family home for seven days. They are not permitted to cross any streams during this time: crossing streams will most likely symbolise moving from one symbolised domain to another. When linking this to the stoning myth, crossing the river may refer to staying in

Figure 8 Coils of thread on *dao* (sword).

heaven rather than coming down to earth, which they will do, it seems, after seven days.

A recap

The Marma system of kinship and marriage, with its elaborate ritual and mythical underpinning, is longstanding and considered to be at the customary core of what it means to be Marma. Much of the symbolism in the marriage ceremony, beginning with the astrological consultations, suggests that a successful marriage is cosmically embedded. Also the preparation of food and the symbolic use of rice and water is significant. A Marma marriage is presided over by a community of actors to make sure that the rules of a Marma marriage have been adhered to. Through the feasts and other ritualised practice, the whole community is drawn into the heavenly ritual space. This section has shown that structure determines the rules and norms, while resources are employed to ensure the smooth re-enactment of culture.

The next section will discuss the significance of the marriage rituals as part of ensuring Marma ethnic continuity.

Discussion of Marma marriage rituals

Marriage rituals that have endured

The ethnographic data reveals Marma marriage rituals that were observed during my fieldwork. The marriage rituals observed by Lewin[13] over 130 years earlier in his 1885 book *A Fly on the Wheel* point to similar but slightly different rituals (Lewin, 1885, pp. 228–229). According to Lewin, when a young man chooses a girl that he wants to marry, his parents also send an envoy to the girl's family, but in Lewin's time the envoy came by boat. The groom's family would ask the bride's household for permission to fasten the boat to the house. During this process, the groom's family would check if the support of the house on the river was firm and whether the boat would have a secure mooring. If the house was old and the supports were weak, they concluded that there would be difficulties in the marriage to overcome. So, over 130 years ago, the marriage process was also concerned about understanding and trying to improve marriage outcomes, although in Lewin's time through the structures and foundations of river homes.

After the examination of moorings, the rituals described by Lewin 130 years ago point to similar processes to those followed at the time of fieldwork.[14] The only difference is that, when the marriage process is considered complete and the couple are married, it is the little finger of both man and wife that are joined, not the hands. Nevertheless, Lewin's account points to a significant fact: Marma marriage process and rituals have largely endured over time, as have the concerns around ensuring a good outcome for the marriage.

The hybrid nature of Buddhist and non-Buddhist interventions

To experience a Marma wedding is to experience elements of several belief systems. Buddhism delivers a protective blessing to the couple as water from pots, situated close to the marriage seat, absorbs the monk's chanting of the *Mangala Suttra* and is then sprinkled over the wedding couple using blackberry or mango leaves. At the same time, the non-Buddhist spirit world is appeased with offerings and prayers to protect the couple from misfortune. The spiritual interventions in a Marma wedding provide a mixture of blessings and appeasement of spirits for the married couple's protection, particularly during the transitional state between engagement and marriage. Thus, religious orders and experts, as well as local spirits recognised by the local Buddhist hierarchy, are consulted at every step because it is believed that the bride and groom are vulnerable to evil spirits.

Marma marriage ceremonies and wedding customs appear to be creolised or hybrid in form: that is to say, they appear as an assembly of elements of Buddhism and elements of pre-Buddhist or non-Buddhist rituals. This hybridity is noted in history. Lewin in 1884 noticed that the Khyoung-tha or river people clans were nature-worshippers, bowing and sacrificing to the spirits of the woods and streams. However, he also perceived the Buddhist elements in their daily lives:

> But in every village the Buddhist "khiong" or temple, was to be found, built of bamboo and mats in the smaller villages, and of solid planks and teak timber posts in the larger communities.
>
> (Lewin, 1885, p. 227)

There is a historical hybridity to Marma ritual practice and, at the same time, the role of Buddhism versus non-Buddhist local practice oscillates in use and significance according to the needs of the group and social context. However, in a Marma marriage ritual, the hybridity is *not* a syncretic fusion of Buddhist and non-Buddhist elements but an orderly succession of separate but interconnected rites. Both Lewin in the 1880s and my observations from recent fieldwork point to a Marma world that is seemingly Buddhist, but brings with it their most important gods, spirits, and practices. Normally the latter play a subsidiary role in most aspects of Marma life. However, it appears that the non-Buddhist interventions dominate in the marriage rituals, while Buddhist elements provide a supplementary layer that invites auspiciousness to the union.

Another component of the hybridity is the role of mythology that sits alongside Buddhist and non-Buddhist interventions. The barricading and stoning in the wedding rites are resonant of the primordial stoning of the first human ancestors by the gods of the sky, where the higher gods in the sky come to earth to stop the lower gods from engaging in sex incestuously. Therefore, the narrative mythically justifies and explains Marma exogamy. Alternatively, part of the myth could also be seen as a re-enactment at the level of kinship and marriage of the first humans breaking free of the sky gods to marry into the earthly realm of humans. In this scenario, bridegrooms (wife-takers) are symbolised as demi-gods of the above who come to earth to become sexual and marry so that wife-takers are of higher rank than wife-givers.[15] The wedding brings about the heavenly union of bride and groom, ritually "creating" divine beings.

The symbolism of *chainga* seems to suggest that, through the fused chicken bone, the couple are merged as one single organism, a part-fused male and female. This provides an indication of the new state of the couple after the wedding ceremony. The couple ritually made into divine beings mean that they avoid the stoning reserved for earthly sexual beings. The expected sexual union is embodied in the fusion of two limbs of the same organism which is witnessed and validated by all, and which then allows the couple to proceed to the next state as sexual beings. Therefore, in accordance with the stoning myth, the symbolism of the ceremony seems to show how the couple can avoid being stoned and have a marriage "made in heaven" that will ultimately be sexual. The message of the ceremony also seems to be that, while exogamy is the customary rule, it is not easy to accomplish since there are cosmic forces about that try to prevent it, as they tried to block the first primordial sexual unions. This explains the recourses to astrology to look for counter-cosmic signs and the considerable work of the engagement and wedding rites to overcome the obstacles.

Agency

The rules are transmitted orally from generation to generation through elders and *medechars*. It is the *medechar*, not the Buddhist monk, who is the custodian of the marriage ritual as he oversees the re-enactment of the rules of marriage and mediates between the couple, the family, and society. He employs syncretic forms as he uses various resources such as a cockerel's fork bones, the *dao* and coils of thread, and pouring water to further validate and protect the marriage. The fork bones engage all members of the audience in the final acceptance of the marriage; the white coils of threads help the couple to enter their new state with safety; and the pouring of water over the hands of the couple – a resource that is familiar to Buddhists – shows symbolically that the community has witnessed the union. The consultation throughout the process helps to validate the union to ensure that the marriage will endure.

Role of chickens

One of the main resources in a Marma marriage is the role of chickens throughout every stage of the process, from courting to engagement and then marriage. Marma experts state that a cockerel symbolises prosperity and a hen represents fertility. From my informant – Shai Shing Aung – I learnt that chicken in marriage symbolises the union of the bride and groom and the wishbone signifies that the bride and the groom are joined together. Often when people stress that a ritual element is a symbol of unity it is because the ritual is acting upon and overcoming pre-states of separation and difference. The early stages and steps of the ritual do indicate separation and difference as all the bits of a chicken are boiled: from head to claws, the good bits and the bad bits. The ritual symbolism of *chainga* seems to indicate that the couple have become like chicken: that they have moved from being separate, from having occupied separate spaces, to becoming as united as the two-pronged bones as part of the chicken.

There are many societies that keep chickens for more than just food. Ethnographic studies show for example that, among the Azande in Africa, chickens are kept mainly for oracular tests, and are only killed for food when hosting important guests (Evans-Pritchard, 1937).[16] In a region closer to the CHT, a study on Chinese folkloric beliefs by Feng (2012) among the Miao in China describes the bird as a messenger of the sun god (Feng, 2012, p. 10). A bird can deliver requests for blessings to ancestors and gods in the supernatural world as it moves between sky and earth, and it carries messages about the future from the supernatural world back to the Miao people. Chickens are good symbolic vehicles for embodying the gods on earth because they are fecund, creating and laying life every day and they are birds seemingly of the sky that spend all their time on the ground. Their very anomaly (in both respects) makes them divine candidates as well as the communicative link between the gods above and the humans below. Therefore, in this sense, chickens are god-like while living among humans. Moreover, Feng discovers what seems to be a similar *chainga* ritual among the Miao in Wangmo County whereby a rooster's wing bone, thighbone, tongue-bone, and eyes are used for predicting the outcome of a marriage.[17]

> The success of a marriage is so crucial to a family or
> a lineage that those affected feel that they have to

> do something to improve the outcome. Chicken in their cultural world has the power to connect the secular world in which they are living and the sacred spiritual world.
>
> (Feng, 2012, p. 19)

The preoccupation for the Marma with potential disorder during marriage stages possibly relates to the systems of patrilineal descent. In this type of community, the sense is that the bride is not a stranger but that her sexuality will potentially create disorder as she enters her husband's family and is consequently seen as crossing boundaries.[18] The bride is a potential carrier of bad fortune to others and the bridegroom is the potential victim.[19] This may create disorder which Douglas describes as symbolising "both danger and power", and that rituals need to be performed that recognise "the potency of disorder" (Douglas, 2002, p. 117). For the Marma and the Miao, using a rooster to predict the future of a marriage and provide protection of the couple through their transitions from one state to another reinforces its mystical function as it helps towards managing the dangers of the liminal phases towards a restoration of family order.[20] Through the work of the wedding ritual, the bride and groom have become a chicken-like earthly unity that has incorporated part of the heavenly above.

Some concluding thoughts

What is remarkable is the enduring nature of the marriage rituals and rules, which were first cited by Lewin as early as the 1880s. These rules and practices have been reproduced over time, with knowledge handed down to elders and embodied in the agency of the *medechar*. Moreover, they constitute the ritual core of being Marma, making up the key elements of a stable and enduring Marma ethnicity.

While the Marma people are internally exogamous, on the boundaries of culture, the outwardly defining characteristic in the Marma world is that it is a Buddhist society. Yet in Marma marriage rituals, the non-Buddhist elements dominate as it expands religious practice with Buddhist elements supplementing it. This hybridity also contributes to the perception of a Marma cultural world of distinctiveness.

However, since daughters can inherit property and even land, out-marriage for daughters is especially problematic for the Marma group as the daughter's inheritance is taken from the family and travels with the daughter to her marriage to another family or outside the community. While this chapter has looked at Marma kinship practices and only touched upon the challenges faced in an environment of change, the next chapter will illuminate how the Marma people tackle challenges to their kinship customs as they work on the boundaries of culture to separate themselves from other groups. It will focus on endogamy rules that help the Marma community to keep Marma culture, land, and religion within its boundaries.

5
Ethnic endogamy
Land, culture, and religion

Over a period of two centuries, the migrating group that came to be known as the Marma intermarried with Arakanese Buddhists during their journey to the CHT. However, during fieldwork, it was clear that the Marma people are nowadays less tolerant towards inter-ethnic marriage as it seems to present a threat to Marma group cohesiveness.

Ethnic endogamy is preferred – that is, the practice of marrying within the Marma community.

The reasons for the shift are anchored in the new realities of the CHT: (a) the changing demographics of the region in terms of the influx of Bengali settlers; and (b) the growing population imbalance in favour of women in the Marma group as a result of protracted civil war and the increasing number of Marma men becoming celibate monks.

In the previous chapter, we have seen how a Marma marriage works within clan exogamy. This chapter will explore how the group strives to conform to overall ethnic endogamy rules, which is the custom of marrying within the limits of a local community or tribe, amid the new challenges in the region. The chapter will provide background to how the boundaries of culture have been maintained, followed by a discussion on the recent stress points with the concomitant threat of out-marriage, concluding with the cultural practices that have been adapted to continue ethnic endogamy within the group.

Ethnic endogamy practices in the Marma group

Naming

From the moment a Marma child is born, he or she receives a name that is uniquely Marma. This name defines the ethnicity of the child and differentiates the child from other children in the CHT. From birth onwards, this Marma name is consulted at crucial moments of a Marma life: from providing clues to the compatibility of individuals for a marriage, to gaining permits to reside or buy land in the Bohmong Circle. Marma naming at birth helps to maintain Barthian boundaries between cultures.

The taboo of inter-ethnic marriage

Since the changing demographics of the CHT, new stress points have been developing on Marma ethnic boundaries. Women traditionally inherit property and goods and sometimes land if there are no male heirs. Moreover, within the Marma community, women can enjoy this inheritance exclusively and independently. But if they marry out, the husbands from another culture could have rights to the property or the inheritance of their wives. Talking to respondents and experts in the field, it became clear that marriage to another tribal Buddhist is acceptable but not preferred while marriage to a Bengali whether Buddhist or

Muslim results in punitive actions such as the denial of property and inheritance rights and quite often social ostracism.

Currently, if intermarriage occurs, there is an order of acceptability: Buddhist Arakan/Rakhine to Buddhist Chakma or other tribal Buddhists are considered acceptable; tribal Christians are the next category that are acceptable; a Buddhist Bengali is unacceptable; and a Bengali Muslim is taboo. This Marma arrangement of marriage preference reveals a strong ethnic endogamy, but on occasion they will intermarry with other tribal people who are Buddhists, as long as they are not Bengalis. Therefore, it seems from this order of acceptability that religion as well as ethnicity are important factors in the taboo on inter-ethnic marriage.

There is no written Marma rule on inter-ethnic marriage, but there exists a "convention" or an ideal that has been handed down from generation to generation and is upheld by the Bohmong office in customary law cases that tackle questions on marriage. For example, while the Bohmong office provides guidance on taboo marriages such as parallel cousin liaisons,[1] it also presides over questions on an inter-ethnic marriage or when a Marma woman or wife has an affair with a Bengali Muslim, both of which are considered taboo.[2]

> There was a Marma couple whose marriage was in crisis. I think the wife may be having an affair with a Bengali Muslim. If she divorces her husband and marries the Bengali, she will lose her rights to the property and she would also be ostracised.
>
> (Interview 17th Bohmong)

The Bohmong and the head clerk are experts on Marma customary law, and through their consultations and interpretations of the rules and conventions around marriage, they uphold customs against inter-ethnic marriage, and as a result, they uphold Marma endogamy rules.

However, the rise of a Bengali settler population and the decrease in marriageable Marma men has meant that the usual stress points on the Marma boundaries of culture have reached an alarming state.

The next section will examine the different issues around intermarriage in relation to ethnicity, religion, and land and the Marma strategies that have emerged in response to this as well as the adaptations on the boundaries of culture that were required to keep them closed.

Contemporary pressures

Demographic changes and the land

The changing demographics of the CHT has long been a sensitive issue. This began with the Population Transfer Programme (1979–1984) with the nation state of Bangladesh, which resettled hundreds of thousands of landless plains families in the CHT. Between 1979 and 1984, approximately 200,000 to 400,000 landless persons were settled in the hill tracts.

Changing population of the CHT

In a census study by Nasreen and Togawa (2002), it is evident that the proportion of the non-hill people has increased in the CHT over time. Their data shows that in 1872, 98.27 per cent of the population of the CHT was made up of hill communities and 1.73 per cent was Bengali. By 1959, the indigenous population had decreased to 90.39 per cent while the Bengali people had steadily increased to 9.61 per cent. Thereafter, the demographics of the region dramatically altered and migration from the plains area was a constant threat to maintaining the separate identity of the hill peoples and their land. The percentage of hill people fell to 59.17 per cent and that of the Bengalis rose to 40.83 per cent in the period between 1959 and 1981. From 1981 to 1991, the Bengali population increased further from 40.83 per cent to 48.66 per cent.

Thus, up to 1930, people not regarded as indigenous to the CHT could not enter or reside within the region without a written permit from the government – the CHT Regulation Rule 52, since repealed. By the year 2011, 51 per cent of the population of the CHT was indigenous and 49 per cent Bengali. This shifting of land from ethnic groups to the Bengali population has created an uncertain future for the communities in the CHT.

During fieldwork, informants were anxious around both the in-migration of Bengali settlers, which was affecting the demographic balance of the region, and also the changes to local land ownership practices. The idea that local land was being lost to or grabbed by outsiders was causing the greatest anxiety. To understand this, the next section will detail the history and background to land ownership in the CHT.

End of the excluded area

The 1900 Regulations Act was originally set up to protect the CHT as an "excluded area" and to prevent outsiders, particularly the dominant Bengali population, from settling there and owning lands.[3]

Thus, the original intention of the Regulations Act was to prevent people from the plains entering the CHT and to block "non-residents" from buying or inheriting land in the CHT.

The Permanent Residency Certificate was first mentioned in Rule 52 of the 1900 Regulations Act:

> If an applicant for a permit satisfies the DC that he is a permanent resident of the CHT, his application shall not be refused except on the grounds that he is an undesirable.

However, since the Peace Accord of 1997, this clause was reinterpreted to allow anyone to purchase land in the Bohmong Circle and beyond, and since a permanent residency certificate is issued at the discretion of local leadership, this is now decided by a Bangladeshi state-appointed district commissioner of Bangladeshi origins. Moreover, all permit requests come to the Bohmong Office as pre-signed by the same representative of the Bangladeshi government. Significantly, in 2009, a Human Rights report stated that "the indigenous people are on the verge of total eviction from their ancestral land" (Kapaeeng Foundation, 2010) as approximately 250,000 acres of land were sold to Bangladeshis in the Bandarban district, illustrating the extent of the transfer of land to those seen as outsiders.

The shortage of marriageable Marma men

Alongside the loss of land to outsiders, an additional trend in the Bohmong Circle has resulted in a new kind of pressure in the region. At the time of fieldwork, interlocutors expressed a growing anxiety over the lack of male marriageable partners for the growing female population. There is a noticeable gender imbalance in the Marma population due to the fact that the CHT region has experienced a protracted 30-year civil war and also because of a large and growing community of celibate monks in the area. As a result, Marma women are not in short supply, but marriageable men are. As one of my respondents explained:

> Not only for a princess, it's very difficult for educated girls. What's going on. It's very difficult to find men to marry.
>
> (Princess Lily, in her early 30s)

The gender imbalance and the lack of marriageable men has added pressure on ethnic endogamy rules. To exacerbate this issue, the stories of women who married outside of Marma culture were on the rise and becoming an alarming new reality.

The main Marma anxiety revolved around the fear that Marma girls would marry Bangladeshi Muslim men. We have already seen in the history of the CHT region that there is an antipathy towards the wider Bengali population. However, since Marma women are fair-skinned, which is associated with great beauty in the region, they are much sought after by Bangladeshi men. This presents a dilemma for Marma society: should a marriage take place with a Bengali Muslim man, a Marma woman's inheritable property will be at risk of eventually becoming part of her husband's assets. Marma girls would hand down their property and inheritance to their mixed heritage sons or, if a Bengali man was accepted into the family, the family would fall under Bangladeshi law – not customary law – allowing the father to own everything that belongs to his wife. Since the Marma system was also part matrilocal, there was also a fear of outsiders living inside the Marma community. In reality, it was more likely that when Marma women did marry out, their husbands would not come to live with the bride's family and the girl would be disinherited to safeguard the family's property. Thus, the anxiety around intermarriage with Bengali Muslim men revolves around the potential loss of culture and land.

Challenging endogamy rules – elopement

A modern-day strategy in the Marma community to force a marriage outside of the endogamy rules is elopement. However, there are elopements that can result in an immediate expulsion from the family. The most controversial elopement is when a royal princess marries a Bengali Muslim or Buddhist. Two young respondents, Prince Kai and Princess Lily, both have sisters who married a Bengali Buddhist and a Muslim, that is, they married outside of their culture and into the "enemy culture". As females, they are seen to be spiritually weak so there was an expectation that their faith would be relegated and that their offspring would become Muslim not Buddhist or more Bengali than Marma. Since there is an unwritten law that disinherits Marma girls if they marry a Bengali, the sisters were disinherited to keep the family inheritance and property in the Marma community.

Kai's sister married a Bengali Muslim but then divorced him. Because she was educated, she was able to work at an NGO and support herself. She eventually married an American Christian. This second marriage and her wealth enabled her to return to Bandarban again and she was accepted back in to the family. Lily's eldest sister – Joy – married a Bengali Buddhist. All her maternal uncles barred Joy from returning to the family house. Joy has a child and lives in Dhaka and has only been allowed to return twice to Bandarban – for the funerals of her grandfather and her brother. During this visit, she stayed with her husband's family since she was barred from her household. When interviewing the mother of Joy, she talks about only having one child left out of three, even though she has another daughter in Dhaka. Although Joy's husband was a Buddhist, it was the fact that he was a Bengali that made Joy experience a "social death" in the Marma community.

There are also examples of alternative outcomes arising from these forbidden unions. In the compound where I lived, the middle daughter of the eldest brother eloped with a Bengali Buddhist. She ran away to live together with her boyfriend for over a year. Her family experienced the shock, shame, and sorrow of this action. There were first whispers and then complete silence around the events as it was no longer discussed. However, almost a year later, the daughter was accepted back into the family with her husband.

These examples from the fieldwork illustrate how the Marma as an ethnic group have rejected Bengali men[4] as suitable marriage partners for their women. There is a sense that ethnic out-marriage will result in the possible loss of property and maybe land. Thus, the demographic changes have challenged Marma endogamy rules and inheritance practices, and instead of making them flexible, the Marma people appear to be resisting this change by tightening the unwritten taboos around inter-ethnic marriage. In order to keep land and property in the

Marma community, marriage in Marma society is focused on reproducing ethnic endogamy. Significantly, women without the prospect of marriage appear to be resigned to their fate to be spinsters, working as local entrepreneurs and traders, in education and for NGOs.

Attitudes to inter-ethnic marriage in Burma

To understand the resistance to inter-ethnic marriage, it is interesting to survey the historical attitudes to similar concerns in neighbouring Burma.

British-instigated migration to Burma

Before hard borders were established, the region known today as Myanmar was a place of porous frontiers and interpenetrating political systems. Added to this fluidity were the imported cultural influences of the British, as the Empire extended its power into the region:

> The British, who took Burma in three stages after 1824, ended nearly a thousand years of unbroken monarchical rule and side-lined the Buddhist clergy, disdaining its central position in society and embittering the Buddhist population. The subsequent importation of hundreds of thousands of Indian workers, who rose to economically powerful positions, compounded fears that Buddhism was under threat.
>
> (Wade, 2018, p. 3)

With the British annexation of lower Burma in 1850, new peoples came to this region from different parts of the British Empire –

India, Malaya, Straits, China – in order to fill administrative and agricultural opportunities and to support the expansion of the Empire's infrastructure. During this period, the British Empire introduced racial classification in order to understand the complex ethnic groups, and this had the effect of stimulating boundary-making between peoples as "once-fluid notions of ethnicity began to calcify into hard distinctions" (Wade, 2018, p. 3). Inevitably, male workers married local Burmese women as these women became the anchors for the migrant families in Burma. However, out of this mingling of groups came a fear in Burma that Buddhism was under threat, and this fed into the anxieties around intermarriage.

Resistance to inter-ethnic marriage

According to Ikeya (2013), as far back as 1939, there are references in Burmese literature to a left-wing nationalist *Kyi Pwa Yei* or Progress group, which presented a diatribe against intermarriage and miscegenation – the interbreeding of people considered to be of different racial types.[5] Ikeya conducted an examination of civil court cases and jurisprudential debates that dealt with marriage, adultery, divorce, inheritance, and adoption in this period, and court cases that gave insights into kinship ties. The legal system at this time was a plural one because of Burma's incorporation into the British Raj in 1826. In this system, family relations and religions were exempted from the civil law of state and made subject to customary law, whether it was "Burmese Buddhist law" or "Mohammedan law" or "Hindu law", depending on which group the person belonged to. Migrant males[6] took precedence in the plural legal system, which resulted in their Burmese wives often being stripped of their customary rights.

Burmese women sometimes voluntarily gave up their equal share in property and the joint custody of children. Some women converted and became subject to Muslim law, which was more favourable to men.[7] There are also examples of women resisting this lowered legal status: apostasy, or the refusal to follow a religion, was documented as one strategy for a woman to revert to her rights as Buddhist; and another strategy was to keep up Buddhist merit-building activities so that her children would benefit in a future rebirth.

Since customary law of the man took precedence over the "personal law" of a woman, there was much anxiety around marriage between a Burmese woman and a foreign migrant,[8] which was only addressed in various laws in 2015, at the time of fieldwork.[9] Even so, the fear around intermarriage is still present in modern-day Myanmar. For example, the political leader – Aung San Suu Kyi – was prohibited from becoming the president of Myanmar due to a clause in the constitution stating that her late husband and children were foreign citizens.[10]

Central to the fear around intermarriage is the loss of land and property and the rights of women. The next section will detail property transmission practices within the Marma context, and how Marma cultural practice protects women from losing access to their inheritance.

Property transmission and protection

Marma inheritance laws

Marma concerns around land and the inheritance of that land will be examined as they are central to why Marma ethnic endogamy is carefully maintained. In the CHT, the Marma people appear to be alone in their concern. According to Lévi-Strauss (1952a) and Ahamed (2004), while marriage is patrilocal among all the groups in the CHT, the Chakma, Kuki, Bawm, and Tanchangya do not allow females to inherit property or land.

There are different interpretations of Marma inheritance or *Am waing* in local literature. According to Lévi-Strauss, inheritance rules distinguish between "male goods" (*iokia waing*), which include house, goats, cattle, and also land, which goes from father to son, and "female goods" (*min ma waing*) consisting of ornaments, jewellery, dresses, spinning tools, fowl, and pigs, which go from mother to daughter (Lévi-Strauss, 1952a, p. 51). Ahamed (2004) claims that both male and female can inherit the hereditary properties of the household, which are classified as two main types: "moveable", which covers agricultural implements, domestic animals, spinning equipment, and ornaments and clothing, and "immovables", which covers land, houses, and trees. According to Ahamed, customary practice dictates that houses, cattle, and agricultural equipment are considered male movables, while female movables are spinning tools, clothing, ornaments, and pigs. The immovable property and paddy lands are distributed equally between son and daughter. If there is more than one son, usually the first born is heir to 50 per cent of the inherited land and property and the other siblings, including females, get a share of the remaining 50 per cent (Ahamed, 2004, p. 128). Khan (1999) posits that since inheritance customs are unwritten, there are many ways in which property and land can be divided; sometimes only the sons inherit from the father the equivalent of the immovables while the daughters inherit from their mothers the equivalent of the movables. In some places, all inheritance can be divided equally with all the children, including the daughters.

The fact that women inherit part of the family's possessions, even land, often surfaces as a source of pride in the community. At the same time, it a source of anxiety because of the risk of losing inherited goods through intermarriage. The main problem arises when unwritten customs that are interpreted in customary law courts come into conflict with the nation state Bangladeshi Muslim inheritance law whereby all of a wife's inheritance comes under the control of the husband. There were many examples during fieldwork of efforts to protect marriages from breakdown and divorce, as well as to protect widows, so that women would not marry outside of their culture and take their inheritance with them. The role of marriage payments in the marriage process is an important step in safeguarding a woman from re-marrying after divorce or becoming a widow.

The role of marriage payments

There are different types of marriage payments that help to keep Marma property within the Marma community. We will also examine how practices have been adjusted as a result of the popularity of the dowry system, which is the marriage payment custom of the majority state.

Marma marriage payments

The Marma marriage process requires the Marma community to witness and approve an important announcement of the marriage payment. This is called *Chameng Than Pwe* (elders) or *Mengla Tun Pwe* (Khan, 1999, p. 156), or "to be put on the path together", and is the formal sitting down of the two families to negotiate the details of the marriage. It is a public event as it always includes either the headman or a village elder, and the family of the engaged couple. It covers the negotiation and announcement of the bride price (and occasionally dowry).

The most significant type of marriage payment in the Marma community is *laphwe* – a bride payment.[11] A Marma bride payment is a gift transferred from the groom's family to the bride and is a share for life that is held with her family and will protect her in widowhood and divorce. It is believed that bride payments contribute to marriage stability as they restrain the wife's family from effecting divorce since they must return the bride payment. The second main type of marriage payment is *lachung* – "to bring with the hand to the bride's family" – or bride wealth.[12] It usually takes the form of ornaments either made from silver or gold that can always be worn by the bride and is a material pledge that the woman and her children will be treated well. The showiness or shininess of the ornaments symbolises the bride's worth to the husband and the community. Groom wealth is also called *lachung* and it can be male clothes and accessories offered by the family of the bride to the family of the groom in an exact mirror image of bride wealth giving. Groom wealth can also take the form of property or land if the groom in a rural setting moves to the bridegroom's family to live matrilocally. The groom's family are compensated for the loss of labour of their son as he moves to the bride's household, but this payment – as with bride wealth – must be returned to the gift-giving family on divorce. Groom wealth is less common in urban areas, where the son's labour is not required in the same way as in rural settings.

Bangladeshi and Burmese marriage payments

In Bangladesh, South Asia, and urban parts of Burma, the dominant form of marriage payment is the dowry,[13] which is also on the rise in the Marma community. A dowry is similar to Marma groom wealth in that it is a payment from the bride's family to the groom's family. Anderson's (2007) analysis of marriage payments over time in Bangladesh reveals some interesting new trends. She highlights the essential difference between bride price paying societies and dowry societies. Bride price societies in South Asia are relatively homogenous with women having a prominent role in agriculture while often being part of a polygamous household. Dowry, in contrast, is found in socially stratified, monogamous societies that are economically complex and where women have a relatively small productive role. Furthermore, she argues that bride prices are relatively uniform within societies and do not vary by familial wealth. Dowries, in contrast, increase with both the wealth and social status of both sides of the marriage bargain.

Spiro (1977) offers a non-economic motive for the preference of bride payment over dowry in Burmese society which is applicable to the Marma group. Of most importance, he says, is prestige (*goun*) for the bridegroom's family and the Burmese emphasis on conspicuous display. For example, while negotiations are private and behind closed doors at the bride's house, a specially composed fanfare at the wedding announces the size and content of the bride price (about 20 per cent of the assets), suggesting that a better name for this payment could be "wealth display" of the bridegroom's family. Equally, the largeness of the bride price serves to raise the status of the bride, which is a gain both for the bride's family in terms of honour and for the bridegroom's family in terms of prestige. When the bride's family are of a lower social status to the bridegroom, they also achieve an enhancement of prestige through the marriage.[14] For the Marma people, since there is a shortage of male marriage partners, adjusting the bride price to the standing of the bride is becoming more of a challenge. Significantly, though, the Marma are continuing to create their distinctiveness from the rest of the nation by following traditions closer to their Burmese neighbours.

Adaptations and strategies

This chapter has so far outlined the contemporary pressures in the Marma community on marriage customs and rules. We have already seen the problems related to a gender imbalance in the hill tracts. In this section, we will take a closer look at some strategies that tackle the concerns, including the raising of a Bangladeshi-type dowry in order to stabilise Marma marriage.

Hybrid marriage payments

For the Marma community, marriage follows Burmese style customs within a Muslim nation state. We have already seen how the influences of Burma and Muslim Bangladesh, alongside an Indian subcontinent-style dowry system, affect the negotiations of a Marma bride price, as there is a wealth of alternative resources available. Marma marriage payments to the bride's family are compulsory – an unbending rule that covers the loss of a woman from her family. With the challenge of a lack of male marriageable partners for women, it appears that there is a growing tendency for Marma families to offer dowries to allure marriageable Marma men to their families, which also acts as an inducement for Marma women not to marry out. There seems to be an increase in dowry-giving by the bride's family, particularly among the richer strata of Marma society, which can be partly explained by these new conditions, and partly by the draw of showy gold dowry fashion in the capital – Dhaka – on the Marma population. This implies that some wealthy members of Marma society are incorporating Bangladeshi customs.

> The wedding process still follows culture and customs but sometimes the decorations are mixed up with Bengali traditions and held in Bengali venues. Actually, it's all mixed up. For example, my mother gave the gift of organic blankets to my wife's family. They were from her father's house and we used them while I was a child too so they were emotionally important to us. In the choice of ornaments, we are still trying to keep to tradition but something has changed, we are now measuring the deference given to them through other people's eyes.
>
> (Interview Shai Shing Aung)

To illustrate this "mixed up" new trend, Figure 9 depicts a marriage that seems to have incorporated both Bengali and Marma elements, with the use of the Bengali wedding colour of red in Marma dress form. The shift seems to suggest that there is an incorporation of new elements in the Marma marriage

Figure 9 Hybrid elements in a Marma marriage: a Marma wedding dress (not a sari) but in red with gold embroidery.

system – an adaptation necessary to help reproduce the Marma population and culture in the CHT.

Polygamous marriages

In the past, the Marma people have adopted polygamous practices within royal families – up to four wives. Marma polyandry, though once common among the royals, is now rare. Polyandry meant in the past that many wives bore more children and therefore there were more divisions of land, which has impoverished the royal family and is less common now due to the financial responsibilities of such an arrangement. I came across one example in the royal family of sororate practice within a polygamous marriage when a senior prince had three wives in total and wives number two and three were sisters. He had married the younger sister of his Tanchangya Buddhist wife. The reason for doing this was because the eldest sister appeared to be suffering from mental health issues, and instead of returning the bride price to the prince's family, the family supplied a younger sister to help in the household and to be another wife to the prince. This younger sister was much loved by the prince and together they had many children.

A recap

These sections have argued that, with fewer potential husbands, there is a greater likelihood that women will marry out in search of husbands, which puts pressure on Marma endogamy rules. The concerns are around Marma women and inheritance and what will happen to property and land that is owned by women when they marry outside of the community. The Marma group are responding to this challenge to endogamy rules by adapting cultural practice. Looking comparatively at Burmese and Bengali marriage practices and inheritance norms, it appears that the Marma lean towards Burmese practices but are also able to incorporate some new elements – Bengali dowry-giving – in order to maintain the singularity of their practice. However, the most direct strategy for tackling out-marriage is the practice of disinheriting girls who marry out, and narratives around this strategy reappeared throughout the fieldwork. This step protects the community from the loss of land to another culture and maintains the integrity of local land ownership.

Final thoughts on kinship, rituals, land, and endogamy

The analysis of ethnographic data on kinship, marriage rituals, and customs reinforces the idea of a Marma society that endeavours to be stable, with structures that are carefully reproduced but which enter into tension with surrounding circumstances when these radically interfere. The Marma community persists with its kinship practice and marriage rules, and with a set of creolised rituals that lie at the core of this practice. Marriage remains the stage in a Marma life cycle where there is a convergence of society's approval, the re-enactment of cultural customs and rules, an astrological interaction with local cosmologies, the spirit world, and Buddhism.

From the Marma endogamy section, we learn how the Marma people maintain their boundaries and difference with other communities outside of the group. It is clear that ethnic endogamy and descent group exogamy go hand in hand in Marma society, driving decisions and choices in marriage as well as being the source of anxieties when they are breached. In Marma endogamy rules, we see a persistence of traditional patterns of internal social distance, separateness, and social cohesion as the principle of ethnic endogamy is rigorously adhered to. The process of maintaining marriage customs and presiding over disputes or breaches in customs links the Marma community to Burmese customary law. We see how ethnic out-marriage is tantamount to ostracisation and this taboo has a strong influence over the population.

Marma inheritance laws and land have become central to Marma preoccupations for maintaining a Marma existence in the area. The encroachments by Bangladeshis into Marma lands have perhaps even strengthened the reproduction of this Marma practice. We also learn that Marma women appear to be bearers of Marma culture and custodians of boundaries (Cahyaningtyas, 2016, p. 6) as a woman's endogamy maintains a group's identity. Marriage payments, mainly in the form of bride price, provide protection for women and help to keep property and land in the Marma community. A divorcee or widow is less likely to re-marry because of the payments and therefore is less vulnerable to a Muslim marriage. However, the growing population of unmarried women has meant that some strategic adaptions have had to be made, showing that flexibility on conventions exist, while the overall system of kinship and marriage remains the same. For example, in order to stimulate wife-taking within the Marma group, Bangladeshi-style dowries are being raised, which is a new alternative element or resource available within traditional practice.

Chapters 4 and 5 have demonstrated the sense of enduring structures and practice with some recent changes absorbed along the way. The reproduction of practice strengthens the boundaries of Marma culture so that the group can maintain its uniqueness in the region. The anxieties around the loss of culture and foothold on the land appear to underlie the impression of a culturally bounded Marma community with a ritual core that is lived out with passion.

6
Migration and settlement

The next two chapters will explore the broader theme of the invention of traditions and their continuities in two different ways: in the present chapter, through the recounting of the history of migration and settlement of the Marma community; and then, in Chapter 7, through the analysis of the meaning-making around material culture. The chapters demonstrate Marma intentionality – in deciding where to settle in the CHT as a migrating diaspora but also in the choice of material culture and the meanings given to it. Both chapters show the different ways or venues through which the group manufacture a sense of being Marma and how they adapt the traditions over time to create a sense of continuity and a distinct culture on the borderlands.

The history of migration and settlement in the CHT is an important part of the history of the Marma group.

As mentioned in Chapter 3, Leach, Sahlins, and Ortner studied their ethnic groups in the *longue durée* – over a long period of time – as part of the analysis of their ethnographical data. This approach provides the opportunity to uncover the processes at work behind reproducing societal structures and the adaptation of those structures to change. In this chapter, we examine the historical *longue durée* of the Marma group, covering the migration of the group from Burma, and the absorption of other communities along the way. The main focus in this chapter will be to understand the hybrid nature of the migrating community and how interactions with powerful forces in the area led to the reconfiguring of the subgroups within the larger group. The key themes therefore shift from maintenance on the boundaries of culture to examining the cultural processes at work from within the boundaries of a group.

The key themes in this chapter are:

- Inventions of Marma culture: the "Marma" label and the royal chart;
- Agency of royal historian and members of royal family in the creation and maintenance of a Bohmong oral tradition;
- Hybridity theories (syncretism) during migration as the group identity moves from hybridity to singularity in the historical *longue durée*; and
- Hybridity theories (Scott's chaos to order-making theories) during settlement to understand place-making activities.

Introduction

There were two relatively recent inventions that have helped to demarcate the Marma group from other groups in the CHT region – the creation of the "Marma" label as the name for the settled hybrid group in the Bohmong Circle and the object of the royal chart.

The ethnic label "Marma"

The community began to call themselves Marma from the late 1950s when the 14th Bohmong applied to the government to change the group's name to "Marma".

Before the 1950s, the ruling powers over the region, mainly the British and Bengalis, used to call the group *Mog* (Buchanan, 1798), or *Mugh* (Lewin, 1885) or *Maghs* (Khan, 1999). However, there is mention of "Ma-ra-ma" as early as 1789:

> This group was commonly known as "Joomea (Mogs)" to the Bengalis of the plain, but their leader Kaung-la Pru [Kong Hla Phru] explained that "the proper name of the Joomeas is Ma-ra-ma, and that they have resided in this Country from time immemorial".
>
> (Buchanan, 1798, p. 91)

Scholars hold divergent views about the etymology of the term "Mog" or "Mugh" or "Magh" and "Marma". Some claim that the word "Magh" is derived from Magdu, a Sanskrit word which means a seabird and by implication denotes pirates (Risley, 1891, p. 29). Khan in his monograph *The Maghs: A Buddhist Community in Bangladesh* (1999) uses the term Magh to collectively cover both Rakhines (Arakanese) of the plains and the Marma of the hills. Khan (1999) and more recently Htin (2015) see both groups as migrants from Arakan into Bangladesh. However, Khan goes on to contradict this position by linking the label of the group "Marma" with the word Myamma, thereby linking the Marma group directly to Burma (Khan, 1999, p. 41).[1]

The blanket term of "Mog", which was applied to the hill peoples, conveyed a sense of lagging behind or being uncivilised compared to their valley counterparts. By taking the name "Marma", it signalled a distancing from any connotation of being uncivilised while linking the group to its Burmese origins.

The royal chart and the faithful followers

Another recent invention is the royal chart that links the group to a specific time, history, and place. The large Bohmong genealogy chart stands as a museum object and represents the undisputed history of the royal family (see Figure 10).

Marma kinship is difficult to define, due to the hybrid nature of the group, which, as we will learn later in this chapter, arose through intermarriage with other Buddhist communities during migration to the CHT. In contrast, royal kinship – as leaders of the Marma community – is well documented and on public display.

The creator of this chart was Maung Nue Sein, the TCI director and presumabbly the designated royal genealogist at the time.

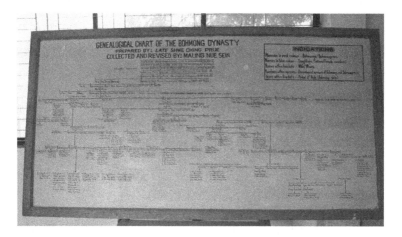

Figure 10 Royal chart at entrance of Tribal Cultural Institute (TCI) in Bandarban.

The creation date is not indicated on the chart. However, the last Bohmong on the chart is the 14th Bohmong. The next Bohmong, Aung Shwe Prue, is on the family chart but not as the 15th Bohmong, which he became in 1998. Moreover, since the chart has not been updated to reflect the subsequent Bohmongs and their families, it is clear that this chart was made in the past and most likely during the lifetime of the 14th Bohmong and before his death in 1996.

The period of the 14th Bohmong's reign was marked by civil war in the CHT, with a peace treaty being negotiated and eventually signed in 1997. Perhaps the chart was created to highlight the strong history of the Bohmong family in the region as a backdrop to war, and the subsequent peace negotiations with the Bangladeshi Government.

The royal chart serves as the starting point for a retrospective analysis of a community's historical journey from Burma to the CHT. The chart covers the period from 1614 to before 1996 and approximately 15 generations of Bohmong leadership. According to the chart, the first four Bohmongs were Governors of Chittagong from 1614 to 1727. It was the 5th Bohmong named Kong Hla Prue[2] who migrated to the hill tracts.

Up until the 9th Bohmong, the Bohmong family was one large family. The succession rules of father to son changed in 1875 as power was transferred instead to the senior most royal member of the family.[3] As a result of this change, the royal family became extended to include three additional branches of families, each headed by a Bohmong. There are a few instances of polygamous marriages of two to three wives in the chart, but it is the 13th

Bohmong who greatly expands the royal family by having 6 wives and 26 children.

When royal members discuss the chart, they relate it to the story of their ancestral origins. The recount a common oral history. The royal family are the descendants of the Prince of Pegu called Maung Sein Pyn, who was the only son of the Emperor of Pegu of Burma. After defeat at the hands of rival kings in the early 1600s, the Prince of Pegu was taken hostage with his sister and "faithful followers". They left the Pegu capital of the Hanthawaddy kingdom[4] to settle eventually in Arakan. The Prince of Pegu became the first Bohmong from 1614 to 1630, and in the following century the descendants of the Prince of Pegu eventually came to settle in the CHT.

This relatively new royal chart acts as a connecting thread that links the current community to its roots in central Burma 400 years ago. From this narrative of the royal family, we learn that the Marma people are a hybrid group made up of royals and faithful followers. It relates the story of the royal family, but through it the whole Marma community – not just the royal family – remember and celebrate their connection to Burma. Moreover, the chart is an object that synthesises different elements of a narrative: it anchors members of the royal family in a glorious past; it intimates their long history in the region; and it implies that royal blood pumps through the veins of an extended network of families.

Thus, individuals working on behalf of the royal family and the oral histories that are triggered by the chart reveal agency working from within the structures of the group to embed a narrative of origins and migration for the Marma community.

The faithful followers

As already noted, the chart covers the genealogy of the royal family. It does not, however, detail the history of the other component of the hybrid group – the "faithful followers" – even though the narrative around the royal chart includes them as an important part of the almost mythical journey.

From various historical accounts, we learn that the followers married into local Arakanese families, and later with other Buddhist communities during their journey to the CHT. Consequently, the assumption is that the present day Marma group are made up of the "faithful followers" who originate from the defeat of Pegu but also includes others who were absorbed along the migration path. These faithful followers who became part of the commoner clans in the Marma group appear to be without genealogy.

Digging deeper into colonial accounts, we learn from Mills that in the early 1900s Kangcha-aong, the headman of Ramgarh *mouza*, told him that his group – the Maghs – had reached the CHT three generations ago and found nothing but jungle with a few tribal people called the Tippera living in the area (Mills, 1927, p. 42).

Visitors to the region have developed their own theories as to the ethnic origins of the commoners in the hybrid group, who came to be known as Marma. Alongside the Bohmong family, Htin (2015) claims that all the hybrid subgroups of the Marma community are from Arakan and not from Burma. He posits that there were different waves of Arakanese migration to Bengal and that the last wave took place around 1794, after the conquest of Arakan in 1784 (Bernot, 1967b, p. 33). The Arakanese settlements during this period were on the coastal areas in present day

Bangladesh such as Cox's Bazar and Patuakhali regions (Khan, 1999, pp. 46–47). These groups, to this day, continue to call themselves "Rakhines" or Arakanese. The other migration wave travelled north in the CHT and the group that settled there became known as "Mong", while those who settled in the south of the CHT became the Marma group.

This claim that the subgroups in the Marma community are originally Arakanese is also observed by some colonial officials at the time. The first traveller to the region, Buchanan, notes:

> These people left their country on its conquest by the Burmas, and subsist by fishing, boat building, a little cultivation, and by the cloth made by their women... The natives of arakan pay no rent for their lands, as every three years they remove and clear away some new spot overgrown with Wood.
>
> (Buchanan, 1798, p. 31)

Hamilton (1825) points out that the old Arakanese community, which had settled in the CHT the longest, faced a new wave of Arakanese refugees following the Burmese invasion of 1784. As a result, two different communities were formed as the older Arakanese community did not want to be associated with the newly arrived Arakanese (Hamilton, 1825, p. 201). In contrast to the Arakan origins position, a rather unusual theory is put forward by Mills (1927, p. 76). Curiously, Mills claims that the faithful followers of the Marma group come originally from Indonesia and that they later became known as Talaings.[5]

Although there is little data on the faithful followers and the other non-royals, it seems that the ethnic origins of the faithful followers – whether Arakanese or Indonesian Talaings – was, and still is, a point of debate.

A recap

It is clear that the Marma label and the royal chart are recent actor-led inventions as they provide an opportunity for the ethnic group to retrospectively narrate and commemorate the history of the Marma from the vantage point of the relative present. Similar to Handler and Linnekin's (1984) invention of culture, the Marma label and chart encompass both continuity and discontinuity, giving new meaning in the present to events and peoples of the past. In contrast, the history of the faithful followers is fragmented and scattered across different sources. However, it is also a significant label, and together with the "Marma" and the royal chart, the "faithful followers" make up the Marma community of today.

A plotted history: The cycle of defeat and triumph

This section will draw on oral histories and the written notes of a local historian and member of the royal family, U Tan Pru. He documented the history of the community until 1950, just before he left the CHT to live in Burma.[6]

In this section, U Tan Pru plots the community's journey, examining their struggles and negotiations with other groups during their migration. The section will cover Marma history from the Emperor of Burma to the Bohmong king; the group's migration journey from Burma to CHT, as they were collectively named "Mog" or pirates by outsiders; the settlement in Bandarban where the group came to be known as the Magh group headed by the Bohmong; to officially being labelled the Marma from the 1950s. It will illuminate the ways in which the Marma deploy narratives and ritual to help define their enduring immigrant identity within the CHT as well as strengthen their distinctness as a group, signalling elements that are bordered, contained, and marked.

It is important to note that the narratives from this group are mostly directed by the royal family, who have both the means and education to invest in it continuously.

According to oral histories, the royal chart, and U Tan Pru's notes, the Bohmong families are descendants of the legendary Emperor Tabin Shweti (1531–1550) of the historical Pegu Empire in neighbouring Burma.

Jesse and Jewel, two young princes in their early 20s, retell the story in the following way:[7]

> It is said that our ancestors were known as Mon of Pegu and they were also the king of that kingdom. It is also said that the throne of Pegu is still in Myanmar.
> You know the first Bohmong. When did he come over here? It was in 1640. He lived in the Arakan state from 1601 to 1640(?) and after that he was sent by the Arakan King over here. Basically, he was defeated by the Arakan king. That's why.

These statements reveal a historical self-understanding among the youngest members of the royal family, but more saliently they illustrate two themes: a glorious past followed by defeat.

Table 2 Chronology of Bohmongs

	Pegu
	Emperor Tabin Shweti (1531–1550)
	Bayin Naung (1551–1581)
	Emperor Nanda Baran (1581–1599)
	The Bohmongs of Chittagong and Bandarban **Chittagong District:**
1	Maung Saw Pyne (1614–1630)
2	Maung Groin Prue (1630–1665)
3	Hari Prue (1665–1687)
4	Hari Kgao (1687–1727)
	Bandarban district:
5	Kong Hla Prue (1727–1811)
6	Thet Than Prue (1811–1840)
7	Thadaw Aung Prue (1840–1866)
8	Maung Prue (1866–1875)
9	Sanaio (1875–1901)
10	Saw Hla Prue (1901–1916)
11	Maung Tha Nyo (1916–1923)
12	Kyaw Zan Prue (1923–1933)
13	Kyaw Zaw Than (1933–1959)
14	Maung Shwe Prue (1959–1995)
15	Aung Shwe Prue (1998–2012)
16	Kyaw Sain Prue (2012–2013)
17	U Chaw Prue (2013–

Defeat

The written notes of Pru describe how the group emerges from an initial defeat to triumph and in stages. The story begins with Emperor Nanda Baran (1581–1599), who ruled over the Pegu empire, being defeated and killed in a battle in 1599 against a formidable coalition made up of the kings of Taungoo, Siam, and Arakan. Pru notes how they fought:

> The emperor king now marched on Ava, being joined with their forces by the kings of Prome and Taungoo. Advancing up the valley of the Sittan river, the army encamped near Panwa. A battle was fought, in which the uncle and nephew, each on an elephant with a small body of followers, engaged in fierce combat.
>
> (Pru, 1950, p. 7)

The city surrendered and the emperor, who was the son and successor of the Great Baran Naung, was made a prisoner of Taungoo, where he was secretly put to death in December 1599.

> Thus perished the last of the emperors of the great Taungoo Dynasty of Pegu which held sway over practically the whole of Burma and Siam with their influence reaching into the remote corners of the Arakan, Assam and distant Indo-China. Never did Burma again rise to such a high pinnacle of glory and military prestige as during that time, and if she did attain it afterwards, during the days of Alaungpra, nothing can surpass the greatness.
>
> (Pru, 1950, p. 7)

In return for his help in the overthrow of Emperor Nandan Baran, the King of Arakan was gifted two captives from the royal family: the Prince of Pegu, Maung Saw Pyne (1614–1630), who was the son of the dead King of Pegu, and his sister Shin Dwe Hnaung, whom the King of Arakan later married.[8] As the group migrated westwards from Pegu to Arakan, the defeated Prince of

Pegu was given a new responsibility as well the gift of new lands. See Figure 11 for the migration path of the group from Pegu, across the Arakan State and to the Chittagong region.

The next section plots the successive journeys of migration from one home to another as a loosely formed group headed by the royal family. The 33,000 "faithful followers" were thought to be members of the royal court of Pegu and, according to Pru, a mix of Burman[9] and Mon.[10] While Maung Saw Pyne lived for 13 years at the Arakanese court, his faithful followers also settled in Arakan. According to Pru, some of the fellow refugees worked under

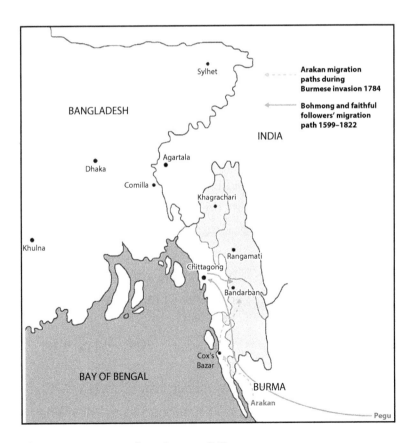

Figure 11 Migration from Pegu to CHT.

the king and the noblemen of the court, while others settled in Mrkhaung and the surrounding districts of the capital. Pru points out that because of intermarriage with locals, it is now difficult to trace the lineage of the faithful followers (Pru, 1950, p. 8).

Military victory

This part of the Bohmong narrative recounts a history of military service to an imperial centre, with victory and the reward of titles.

In 1614, the Arakan king sent Prince Maung Saw Pyne, who had become his brother-in-law, to Chittagong, which was then part of the Arakan province.[11] Prince Maung Saw Pyne developed a reputation as a wise governor and was surrounded by "able counsellors" (Pru, 1950, p. 9). At this time, the Portuguese were repeatedly attacking the Arakanese settlements. Maung Saw Pyne decided to fight back and collected an army, including some of his Bengali allies, and successfully removed the Portuguese pirates from the area in 1620.

> For this victory, he was honoured by his brother-in-law, the king of Arakan, with the title "Boh Mong" which means King of Generals or Commander-in-Chief. This is the title commonly written as "Bohmong". After this Portuguese defeat he ruled the country, without further serious interruptions, till his premature death in 1630 AD.
>
> (Pru, 1950, pp. 9–10)

Similarly, 50 years later, the Bohmong, Hari Kgao (1687–1727), was determined not to give up Chittagong to the new enemy of the time – the Mughals. When a new dynasty was installed in Arakan,[12] Bohmong Hari Kgao was able to regroup troops and eventually defeat the Mughals in 1710.

> For this brilliant victory, he was conferred the title of "Bohmong Gree", which means Great King of Generals. This title was hereditary and affirmed many times afterwards.
>
> (Pru, 1950, p. 12)

The titles of "Bohmong" and then "Bohmong Gree" appear to have reinstated the leaders of the community to a former glory. However, this glory only came after a cycle of successive struggles and defeat against an ethnically different other – first the Portuguese and then the Mughals.

The journey to the CHT

Another theme that is covered in the oral and written histories is the history of displacement and the long troublesome journey to the CHT. Kong Hla Prue (1727–1811) – the same Bohmong who met with Francis Buchanan – like his two predecessors, also struggled to regain possession of Chittagong and, after several attempts, was forced to retire to Arakan again in 1756 and seek shelter at the Arakanese Court (Pru, 1950, p. 13).[13] In 1760, the East India Company ended the Mughal's control of Bengal and Chittagong. On returning to his former territories in the South of the Chittagong Division in 1774, Kong Hla Pru discovered "the Mogul power declining and that the British ascending" (Pru, 1950, p. 13). For the next 30 years, Kong Hla Prue led "a wandering life" (Pru, 1950, p. 12), travelling in search of a permanent home. As he moved deeper into the hill tracts, he left followers behind at each place that he stopped.[14] While slowly working their way north and battling with local "wild tribes", they entered the Sangu Valley and settled at Subalok in 1798. They stayed there for seven years, but finding the place unsuitable, in 1804 they moved a few miles further up the valley to *Furahou Koiyn*, or "Plain of Old House Site", as it came to be called afterwards. During this period, life in the hill tracts was perilous due to constant assaults from the "savage tribes".

> [It] was a wild region…with deep narrow valleys and steaming jungles in which lurked deathly malaria and the terrible head hunter…The struggle for bare existence and the atmosphere of constant danger with which they were surrounded was, as a matter of fact, a far cry from the courtly and polished life led in Arakan.
>
> (Pru, 1950, p. 14)

A colonial administrator from that time, Lewin, describes the danger in similar terms:

> Bah! What is a tiger! The valley below into which we were going was full of human tigers.
>
> (Lewin, 1885, p. 178)

Once settled, Kong Hla Prue was the first Bohmong to make a treaty with the British and come under their influence and protection. He came to oversee all the territories along the river Karnaphuli to the south until the Kingdom of Arakan and divided his followers into four *ackoos* (*mouzas*) and 16 *toins* (villages). To each *ackoo* and *toin* he appointed one *achooshin* (headman) and one *toinshin* (*karbari*) as leader. This hierarchy made it possible for Kong Hla Prue to assert his authority over his people and extract revenue on behalf of the British. In return for collecting tax for the British, the Bohmong and his people received the protection of the British powers in the region. When the Bohmong died, his eldest son, Thet Than Prue (1811–1840), made an agreement in 1820 to pay tax to the British Government on cotton production in the area. Finding the site of their home too small, Bohmong Thet Than Prue moved his headquarters to the present site, Bandarban, in the year 1822 (Pru, 1950, p. 18).[15]

The following Bohmong, Thadaw Aung Prue (1840–1866), was noted as a harsh and ill-tempered Bohmong. Some of his relatives fell out with him, collected a large number of followers and family, and left Bandarban to establish a rival community in Lama on the Matamuri River or moved north. When Thadaw Aung Prue died in 1866, one of his brothers – Maung Prue – with his family and followers returned to Bandarban from the north (Pru, 1950, p. 18). The same year, families from the Matamuri river also came back to Bandarban. The Bohmong's group came to be known as the Rigiesa clan (also known as Regratsa),[16] while other clans, notably the Palangsa clan (also known as Palatine), later to be headed by the Mong *Raja*, moved up into the CHT by another route.

Thus, in the 1950s, U Tan Pru points to a hybrid group made up of faithful followers, Arakanese people, and the Bohmong family. They came to the CHT together, splintering off due to internal group conflict but then coming back together again at different points in history. The next section will detail the difficult conditions in the hill tracts that led the hybrid group to be further subordinated to British influence.

Pact with the "friendly tribes"

Life in the CHT proved to be difficult as various Bohmongs suffered attacks from the Lushai who lived in the upper reaches of the Karnaphuli river and as far as the Lushai Hills in Assam. In order to protect their new settlement, various Bohmongs made a pact with friendly tribes against the offensives from the Lushai, while the town of Bandarban was slowly establishing itself. When Maung Prue assumed the Bohmongship in 1866, raids by bands of Lushai were almost a weekly occurrence.

> They were a troublesome tribe, still unsubdued by anyone, and the British found it rather difficult to check their marauding excursions into the plains. To end these raids, a punitive expedition was sent against them.
>
> (Pru, 1950, p. 21)

Successes were only temporary and within a few years the Lushai were again on the war path. When a young Scottish girl – Mary Winchester – was captured and taken hostage by the Lushai in 1871, she was rescued by a British campaign called the Lushai expedition of 1872.[17] This campaign resulted in the subjugation of the "savage" tribes to British control in the region.

Although the Bohmong worked with the British to maintain peace in the CHT,[18] U Tan Pru also conveys the Bohmong's distrust of British influence in the area. Through his writing, Pru claims that the British had wanted complete subjugation of all tribes in the area and, towards this end, had started to control and limit the powers of local leaders.

> The Chiefs did not like this, nor the people appreciated the idea of a white foreigner ruling over them... A series

of encounters then followed between particular bands of people and the government. But owing to lack of unity and leadership it frittered away without achieving any result. From then onwards, the Chiefs and people have been continuously fighting a losing battle against British injustice and enduring the high-handedness and petty insults of their agents in The Hill Tracts.

(Pru, 1950, p. 21)

To this day, the Rigiesa clan are descendants of the Bohmong-led group. It is through his rights as clan chief of the most numerous of the Magh clans that the Bohmong was able to oversee *jhum* tax collecting rights over large swathes of the Bohmong Circle, including other groups that already lived in the area.

Discussion
Agency

In the Marma group, a series of "actors" created a world in their own terms by instilling it with order, meaning, and a new value – from the unknown actors that began the narrative of the origins in Pegu at the time of Hutchinson and Mills, to the historian's handwritten notes from the 1950s, written at the same time as the group was named Marma, and to the architect of the royal chart. The other actors are the Arakan king and the British, who acted as protectors of the community as they journeyed across difficult and unchartered terrain. But also as foe, since protection of the community came at the price of subordination and constant intervention.

Oral history

During fieldwork, the two young princes repeated the Bohmong history as written down by U Tan Pru: the same main facts that elaborate on the important influence of the royal family as part of a bygone historical period. An influence that still lingers on and is embedded in titles and privileges that U Tan Pru, occupying a prominent place in the royal family, is himself part of.

In U Tan Pru's portrayal of their history, it is as if a diachronic succession of events was simultaneously projected on the screen of the present in order to reconstitute piece by piece a synchronic order which is later substantiated by the roster of Bohmong names embodied in the royal chart. To add weight to Pru's written recount of the group's oral history, he refers to the colonial records of Lewin and Mills. All three corroborate the ideas of an epic defeat and journey of a distinct group of people who have settled in an area with British patronage, practising a culture that has mythical elements, and emphasising the group's connections with a glorious past. All three agree on the point that the British supported the community in order to stabilise the area for tax collection. However, U Tan Pru also expresses his distrust of British interference in his community.

Circularity and syncretism

These sections have plotted the numerous and repetitive defeats and triumphs of the community – which no doubt contribute to their contemporary identity – as well as the continued subjugation of the group, first under the Arakan king and then under the British. From the history of the group, we see a repetitive cycle in the structures in the long run.

Migration begins from the east in Pegu towards the west in Arakan, then north towards Chittagong and finally northeastwards towards Bandarban (see map in Figure 11). The effect of the circularity of migration and the repetition of experience creates an impression of continued struggle and defeat. Sometimes glory, but with the ultimate triumph embodied in a peaceful settlement in the CHT.

What is being conveyed by this narrative of nobility, war, defeat, migration, incorporation of groups-along-the-way as followers, further war, defeat, migration? It seems that the Marma are a hybrid group who are destined to move further and further away from their origin, never becoming truly indigenous and always retaining a separateness that is rooted in history. Consequently, the maintenance of a strongly bounded ethnicity, identity, and difference appears to be about perpetuating this history and remaining part of it. Moreover, the retelling of this history underlies the Marma's strong presence in the CHT, as the body-politic and society of a foreign nobility.

Encounters with "the other" and entanglement

Moreover, interactions with powerful outsiders resulted in manifestations of indigenous foreignness within the Marma group. Sahlins' study of the Sandwich Islanders (1981) contributes to this understanding as he illustrates how a Polynesian community incorporates aspects of the powerful outsiders. This Polynesian community already had an established society and cosmological belief system and were enveloped by their culture, and when they acted upon their culture, they were acting from within it, not from outside it.

In contrast to the Sandwich Islanders, it was the Arakan king – an outside power – who guided the culture of the migrating group by restoring the displaced royal prince to the honoured status of Bohmong. When the migrating group arrived in the CHT, the hybrid group assessed the tribal cultural practices of the CHT that were already there and made a decision to align themselves with the British against the Lusai tribes. In effect, as a group that was new to the CHT, and with the help of an alternative British Empire schema, the hybrid migrating group were able to formulate a culture in opposition to the Lusai.

The hybrid nature of the group is revealed as royal leaders and the subgroup of faithful followers form a group with new people joining along the migration path. The membership of the elementary unit was in flux, as was the very existence of the unit itself. But fluid as they were, these elementary units were the only building blocks available to the royal lineage that led them. From the late 1880s, the subgroups splinter off and then come back together again. Although the reasons for the fragmentation of the group revolved around disputes in leadership, there is evidence that the turning point for the hybrid group, when they started to bury their differences and to come together as one group, may have been triggered by the dangers of being isolated from others in the hostile region of the CHT. The group is then collectively seen as one community of Maghs led by the Bohmong king (Mills, 1927, p. 69).

With historical data of this nature, it is challenging to find examples or insights into the processes of assimilation when each band of newcomers, with their imported new cultural elements, join the group.

The next section covers Pru's notes and my fieldwork data on the challenges of rooting the community in their new home of Bandarban as they define the boundaries of their community against the marauding "other".

Settlement and defining new mythical boundaries

The Sangu river

> There we were at last, far away from civilization, on the banks of a new river, which the Roaja informed me was the Rigray Khyoung, or, as the Bengalis called it, the Sangu River, which flowed to the sea through the territory of a potentate styled the Bohmong.
>
> (Lewin, 1885, p. 152)

The new home of the Bohmong-led group consisted of a thousand houses stretching along the banks of the Sangu river[19] and came to be known as Bandarban. When the community first arrived in the area, they underwent a process of defining and protecting the boundaries of Bandarban with spirit shrines. These shrines were set up on the edges of the forest and along the banks of the Sangu River,[20] which plays an important and sacred role in the Marma community.

Securing the boundaries of the community

In the Bohmong Circle, as in most Southeast Asian polities, the relationship with the world of *nat* spirits plays an important role in local cosmologies. In the Marma community, the legends around defining the boundaries of the settlement focus on the help and protection provided by the *nat* spirits to protect the new settlement from misfortune and attack from outsiders. A series of legends are recounted to provide background as to why boundary setting was necessary.

Legend of the cholera outbreak

According to local legend, there was a cholera outbreak when the group led by the Bohmong first arrived in the area. In response to this, the astrologer advised the Bohmong to worship the *nat* spirits to protect the town. The Bohmong Thet Than Prue duly created four shrines sometime after the 1820s to mark the boundaries between his kingdom and the outside world and to honour the different *nat* spirits of the area. When the shrines were built, the dying stopped.

Legend of the coffin stuck in a tree

Another legend is recounted which reaffirms the community's work on boundaries and shrines for worship. In 1840, when Bohmong Thet Than Prue died, his coffin was kept in state in preparation for his cremation. However, a heavy rain fell that was so severe that the river burst its banks and completely inundated Bandarban, forcing the people to seek refuge in the neighbouring hills. The coffin, which was in the house at the time, was carried away by the current but was caught securely by the top branches of a tree under which the Bohmong's wife was cremated near the old village site. When the water receded, the coffin was brought down and cremated on the spot and a shrine was built to mark its significance (Pru, 1950, p. 15).

The four spirit shrines

Consequently, Bandarban is protected by four *nat* shrines, which allow the community to appease the *nat* spirits of the river and the forests so that the community can live in peace or *chaing* alongside other tribes.

See Appendix E for a map of Bandarban with numbered shrines.

1. **Champa and bodha tree near saw mill – North Chengabaan:** This is the home of the tree spirit. The 5th Bohmong was worried that the original champa tree would die so he allowed a bodha tree to grow there as well and both trees are now intertwined. This place is also close to the old cremation ground, between the edge of the town and the beginning of the forest.
2. **Water shrine on Sangu (West) – Ujani Ghat:** This comprises two shrine structures built from bamboo which mark a point in the bend of the river for *kyang pwe cha* (river worship). This point is where spears and *Palang Makey Dong* (gun shots) from the other side of the river resulted in bullets falling into the waters within a specific range. The point marks the safe boundary in the river from gun shots and spears.
3. **Below bridge and to the left of Upper Ghat:** This is the point where the Marma village ends and foreign lands begin. Again, a bamboo structure in the river is built for worship.
4. **Bodha tree:** On the way to the tennis courts, to the left of the police station. Here, there is also a Bodha tree, signifying the edge of town and overlooking the valley.

The history of the installation of the four shrines is remembered every year during the New Year Water festival celebrations in April, when the Bohmong or a male representative of the royal family leads an all-male procession, with one male representative from each household. A band of musicians and music accompanies the entourage as it walks with swords and parasols and visits each shrine. The procession starts at the Saw Mill (1), then moves to the river "fire shots" shrine (2), along the bazaar road to the bridge and water shrine (3), and then up to the police station to the final tree shrine (4). Offerings are made at the shrines of sweet-tasting food: rice popcorn, banana, coconut, biscuits, and sugar cane. At each stop, the Bohmong office reads scripts from a book recounting the story of how they came to Bandarban and created the boundaries and shrines to protect the community.

The Bandarban edict: Boundary maintenance
The edict

The shrine boundary of Bandarban was an important conclusion to the community's migration story as it protected the group from their first encounters with the dangers beyond their town – whether in the form of wild animals or hostile tribes. However, Marma beliefs around protecting the boundaries of the settlement have been recently reiterated and embodied in local practice. There is an edict that a Marma person cannot die far away from their home as they believe that a dead body is a vessel that is vulnerable to a potential occupation by an evil *nat* spirit. The edict was put together in order to protect the people in Bandarban from outside evil spirits and has been perpetuated by four generations of Bohmongs and enforced by the local leaders – the headmen of the districts and the *Kabari* leaders of villages within those districts.

This edict originates from the time of the 14th Bohmong and during the liberation war (1970s) when there was a flood and, at the same time, an outbreak of cholera and typhoid. The story recounts that a Bawm tribal man went to hospital during the floods. He died in Chittagong city, but when his body returned to Bandarban the floods rose up and swallowed the town. The elders of Bandarban held a meeting with the Bohmong and his headman.[21] The elders claimed that, during the journey home from Chittagong, the dead body was possessed by evil spirits and that this had caused the floods. They received permission to offer the Bawm man's body to the river to appease the angry water spirits. As the body was thrown into the river, the floods receded. Since this incident, it has become a commonly held belief that, in order to prevent an epidemic, dead bodies need to be kept in their place of departure to the next life.[22] For example, if a person becomes seriously ill and dies in hospital – outside of the town's boundaries – then their body will not be allowed to have a Buddhist wake and return to Bandarban. Instead, the body is transported directly to a grave outside the town's boundaries.

As demonstrated in this relatively new edict, the four shrines have a strong grip on the population: it seems to not only convey the importance of the boundaries of the town in protecting the people within, but also to reveal the potential destructive power of local *nats*. Once the onslaughts from other tribes slowly receded, the community seems to have transferred the fear of attack to evil *nat* spirits that live outside the boundaries of the town. Protection has been an important theme as first the community were protected by the Arakan king, then the British and now the *nat* spirits in a hostile Bangladeshi landscape.

Interestingly, the *nat* spirits hold the capacity to be both good in that they provide peace and protection – especially during marriage rituals – but also capable of causing disorder and harm.

Although the group conceive their difference in the hills in terms of their foreign origins, hence the stress on migration, their ethnicity is not one of rootedness. Indeed, the practice of bounding territory with shrines that make up borders and keep evil spirits out contrasts strongly with ancestor shrines and rites that other groups have which stress and cultivate strong links with "the land". In many ways, the Marma relationship with the land is unique. Their land is primarily elsewhere but they have cultivated over time a bounded territory in the CHT where ritualised roots have developed over time.

Purposefulness and place-making

It is useful to look through Scott's (2005) lens at this hybrid group to understand the shrine-building and edicts relating to the new settlement. We have already seen that the royal family are a dynastic elite that originates in Pegu and draws in followers during the migration to Bandarban. When they arrive in Bandarban, they feel themselves to be a single group that demands isolation from the dangerous natural environment. As with Scott's theory, the hybrid group constitutes chaos, but when the group meets the external setting of chaos, for example the unchartered jungles of the CHT, the empty land or "vacuity" and space are areas of chaos that need "place-making" activities. In fact:

> The production of locality is… one of the most tangible registers in which people strive to bring order out of chaos.
>
> (Scott, 2005, p. 198)

This semantically empty land triggers an identity-making process within the hybrid group which entails the hybrid subgroups uniting against the chaos of the external – the unruly tribes, the onslaughts, the diseases that inflict the group – to create a boundary around their new land. During this process, they define who is allowed to live within the boundaries and who is excluded, and this helps the group to live together in clearly grounded polities. Moreover, the process of order production is periodically revisited, as can be seen through the Bandarban edict. Therefore, in this section we see hybridity at work as the group slowly becomes singular in response to external changes in the environment, and also due to a process of differentiating the group from others in the area. As internal order was created, the diaspora began to settle and develop roots in the region from the 1830s onwards.

Again chaos: The decline of Bohmong power

Almost 200 years after the first settlement and place-making activities in the Bandarban region, chaos has been reintroduced into the group and the region. Central to this are the royal succession disputes.

We learn from the history of the Bohmong family that they received the gift of land: first in Chittagong from the Arakan king and then in the CHT as it became part of a protectorate of the British Empire. Every Bohmong displayed their right to rule over the land by building palaces called *rajbaris*. This section will explore the importance of the royal palaces to the Marma people and what one photograph of a *rajbari* has come to represent and convey in terms of their past and future.

Destruction of a royal palace

Every Bohmong family was required to build a *rajbari* or royal palace and, as a result, Bandarban is populated with many different palaces. They were originally made from bamboo and rebuilt every year, but the first cement building is still standing in Bandarban and belongs to the 14th Bohmong. The separate palaces of the 15th and 16th Bohmong are more modern and currently hold a commanding position in the centre of the town. Because the population of the town is estimated to be only about 32,000, it is remarkable that there are still three visible palaces remaining.

In direct contrast to the reverence for the royal family that emanates from the royal chart, I observed a counter-sentiment that emerged from a recent selling of royal lands to Bengali investors. The palace and land in question had been demolished in 2012 and was located at the king's pond. During my first months in Bandarban, I was shown photos of the palace before its destruction, as I listened to the collective anxiety that seemed to be triggered by its loss.

Two younger princes in their 20s described the situation of the destruction and loss of the 13th Bohmong's palace in the following way:

Figure 12 Rajbari of 13th Bohmong in the distance.

> At that time, the kings had elephants and old vehicles. But now you can see everything's ruined. And not the same as before. There was a huge wall over that side and guards and all ... when we were young, the building was still here. Both of us lived in here. His father, his mother, my grandfather, my grandmother ... Well it was really a nice place. On the ground floor, there was a big hall of rooms and other rooms where we could play six-a-side football.

When asked what had happened, this was the explanation offered:

> Basically, too many descendants, too many successors. Infinite needs... it is still a huge family so everyone had to be individually given a piece of land from here. So it had to be sold and demolished. There was no choice.

According to the current 17th Bohmong:

> Money is divided to all family people. My grandfather (13th Bohmong) had 6 wives, 14 sons and 9 daughters. Nothing now…my grandfather said I am the last king… my grandfather said there will be a king but he'll be nothing.

The sale had arisen due to too many royal family members inheriting royal lands. With further prodding, I discovered that the royal succession rules were behind this problem as it had widened the network of royal families and thereby put pressure on royal land ownership.

Shrine boundaries breached

This palace belonged to the 13th Bohmong, who had had the largest and most impressive *rajbari* to house his family from six wives. After his death, his practice of polygyny had eventually resulted in a large family that was financially weak. Members of the royal family resorted to selling off valuable land to the highest bidder in order to continue living in the region. Significantly, the sale had happened after the peace treaty of 1997 that had enforced land registration, which in turn had triggered a scramble for land ownership by Bangladeshis in the CHT. As a result, the royal lands were sold to people outside the community, breaching the shrine boundaries and causing a huge anxiety in the Marma community. Moreover, the consequence of having a large extended royal family has meant that some members of the royal family are now financially weak, and since wealth is considered to go hand in hand with power, the royal family has recently experienced a diminishing of respect from some other non-royal members of the community.

Another incident occurred during the time of fieldwork, which was hugely distressing for all, including myself. A young boy who frequently visited the compound where I lived had drowned mysteriously in the shallow waters of the Sangu river while playing with his friends. After his death, the narrative that circulated in the Marma community was that the *nat* spirits were angry with the little boy's family for selling off land to Bengalis and therefore claimed his life.

This theme of loss of land to another group seems to dominate and underpin much of the Marma anxieties encountered during fieldwork.

Competition and conflict at the apex

With every new Bohmong come new approaches and fresh ideas, which have the potential to increase the contribution to the community. Knowledge and experiences of kingship and interactions with government and the other circle chiefs are shared with the wider family, making many members experts in government and customary law. Furthermore, on becoming the Bohmong, the whole family gains influence and leverage. However, with every new succession, existing royal lands are allocated to the new king and his family, causing even more pressure on royal land tenure.

The Bohmong family, as a result of the "fair" succession rules, has experienced an increase in rivalry, resentment, and a constant striving to come out on top. Added to this is a decline in wealth of the Bohmong family: if all royal members inherit equal shares of a given amount of land, it will not take long before each person's plot is too small to support a family. Thus the inheritance rules of the Marma group have produced a decline in the standard of living for the royal family as a whole.

This section has illustrated that, towards the end of the cycle of the history of this group, the stretched structures of the system seem to have reached a point of exhaustion, reverting the group back to a sense of uncertainty.

A recap

This chapter has revealed the various phases of the community's migration to and settlement in the CHT. From this chapter, we learn about the defeat in Pegu and that a group formed around the surviving royal heirs. Then followed a cyclical process of war and defeat as difficulties were overcome in stages through triumphs in military battles. Moreover, the group had migrated from a splendiferous royal court to the savage lands of the CHT,[23] and during that journey, the leaders emerged as Bohmongs who became warriors, peacemakers, and diplomats, leading the migrating group to its new home. The group ultimately re-established itself again to a former glory through the Bohmong Circle, headed by a Bohmong leader and with the protection of the British and the local *nat* spirits who also held the potential for harm, unless appropriately appeased.

We learn that the community is a hybrid group that at the same time strives to display a distinct ethnic identity that sets itself apart as a group in the CHT. The syncretism theories of Herskovits (1937) shed some light on the adaptation process of this migrating community, as it seems that the closer the group are to their Burmese origins in the early stages of migration, the less their ancestors go out of their way to be endogamous. In contrast, the closer they are to the CHT, the more the group emphasise their boundaries, the more they become endogamous and the more they become a single ethnic group. The Marma people themselves have over a historical *longue durée* synthesised the themes to stress a continuous existence in the region and to demonstrate that there is a thread that connects the Marma of today to Burmese times.

The Marma unique oral history specifies their distinctiveness as neither diasporal nor indigenous but something along the lines of diasporal-becoming-settled, while pointing to their irreversible presence in the CHT through the boundaries of the four shrines and the building of royal palaces.

Early external British intervention on succession rules has resulted in a multi-family dynasty which increased the pool of royals so that different branches of the royal family have at some point in the history of the Marma group become part of the ruling family. This expanded royal family have been recipients of Marma oral history and played an important role in maintaining and reproducing its narrative. However, with the rising Bengali settler population in Bandarban town, the integrity of the boundaries of the town has been breached. If we employ Scott's chaos and production of order concepts to these recent events, it will appear that the once ordered hybrid group has been thrown back into chaos again.

This chapter has looked at migration and settlement of the group and covered some important objects – the royal chart and the photo of the *rajbari* – that embody the different narratives of the group. The next chapter will turn to a further selection of material culture of the group by focusing on specific events and objects that help to further define and differentiate the Marma group from their neighbours.

7
The invention of Marma material culture and ceremonials

The chapter on migration and settlement revealed the changing form of the hybrid group, as the group mainly made up of the royal family and faithful followers was known as the Magh group led by the Bohmong. From the 1950s, they became known as a single ethnic group called the "Marma". The further the migrating group travelled away from Burma, the more the group became endogamous (custom of marrying within a community) and a stable, ascendant power. The royal chart as an object within Marma material culture enabled the recounting of the group's narrative, which stressed the connection with Pegu while at the same time reiterating their long history in the CHT region. In contrast, the photograph of the *rajbari* was an object that signalled the beginning of a loss of royal power and land ownership in the CHT, as well as the trigger for an increasing uncertainty around the group's future in the region.

There are other narratives being told that do not necessarily follow a historical timeline but contribute in different ways to the overall progression of the Marma narrative. Marma identity and tradition is created and bolstered by material objects, commemorative rituals, and symbols of kingly power. This chapter will explore in more detail the significant role of material culture in the Marma community and how it is able to convey simultaneously a sense of a distinct culture, continuity over time, the unchanging essence of the group, and, most significantly, the purposefulness in Marma identity-making.

The chapter will study the processes behind the inventions of Marma culture that, through constant reinterpretation, achieves a continuity with the past. This chapter will illustrate the crucial role of the royal family in developing the intimate connection with the recounted past through the deployment of both royal objects and royal bodies in ceremonies, supporting the Bohmong narrative that began with migration and settlement. The chapter will also examine the cultural entanglement and syncretism embodied in the objects and the ceremonies that help to bring together the subgroups within the hybrid community.

To summarise, the following topics will be covered:

- kingly power through the narratives around the Bohmong sword;
- the annual re-enactment of the tax collection ceremony – the *raj punya* (sacred festival of the royals), which combines elements of kingly shininess and authority; and
- the coin garland, which is an object of value to the non-royal members of the group. It symbolises value and shininess as it strings together the universal kings while primarily serving as a form of bride price or bride wealth for the protection of women.

The observations in the chapter are based on my interpretation of the data collected and the conversations around the objects with different members of the community.

The concept of shininess

Alongside the spinning looms,[1] bamboo shrines to *nat* spirits, and the Buddhist structures in the CHT, Marma material culture is distinct from other groups as it draws heavily upon the concept of shininess or radiance to emanate power from the apex. There are many Marma words that convey this sense of shine. *Taukte* and *lanre* are two similar words that mean shininess or radiance, respectively, and when *al* is added in front of the words, the phrase conveys a sense of added or increased shininess. Another term – *alan raung* – has the combined meaning of "the shininess of power". According to my respondents – the royal princes, and the elders – and colonial visitors to the region, the preoccupation with radiance and shininess in the group appears to be connected to the Pegu of the 1600s. Pegu was then a highly developed Burmese city with wide streets, fabulous golden pagodas, and a rich and sophisticated court with its much-esteemed retinue of white elephants. In 1584, Ralph Fitch,[2] a merchant of London visiting Burma to ascertain products and enquire about trade, described Pegu – the capital of the region – as being grander and more extensive than London (Farrell, 2007–2008, pp. 16–18).[3] Moreover, the oral narratives of the Marma list the spoils of war and symbols of royal power that accompanied the royal family after their defeat in Pegu: weapons, gold, and four white elephants. The list of spoils of war were repeatedly recounted by the royal respondents during my fieldwork, which reinforced the symbolic power of this first generation of Marma material culture.

The sword that shines

On my first visit to the home of the leader of the Marma group – the 17th Bohmong[4] – I was shown a gallery of photographs of the various Bohmongs in their royal regalia, with the first image dating back to the 1930s. Each Bohmong appeared to be carrying the same sword with ornate hilt which was part of their ceremonial dress (see Figure 13). There was also a gold chain which was believed to be a gift to the Bohmong from the British who helped the Lusai expedition of 1871 to 1872.[5]

The 17th Bohmong described what he knew about the significance of the sword:

> I want to show you the sword that we have long ago. We hand over this sword from one to another. I think this is during British time. British offer this sword to the *Raja*. I'm the 17th Chief still carrying this regalia and hand over to the next. When I die, this will go to the 18th king of Bandarban... See there the architect of the sword. So nicely flowers here and there. ...See the head, dragon head...only the king can carry the sword, can hold the sword.
>
> (Interview 17th Bohmong)

When the 17th Bohmong recounted the history of the sword, he stressed that the sword was connected to the hostage prince of Pegu who was made governor of the land to the west of Arakan (Chittagong). This prince had the opportunity to regain his former glory by defeating the Portuguese pirates. He became

Figure 13 Kingly swords

Left: the Bohmong sword, thought to be a gift from George V. **Right**: swords of the faithful followers, stacked under the bed of the present Bohmong. These swords are currently carried by the bodyguards of the Bohmong during ceremonial events.

the first Bohmong of this dynasty and, according to oral history, he was also the first ruler to receive a sword as a gift from the King of Arakan. From then on, according to the 17th Bohmong, each new ruler inherited this kingly sword. However, the first sword, gifted by the Arakan king, was lost at some point and the current sword, as seen in the photo gallery in Figure 14, was thought to be a gift from George V when the CHT region became part of British India.[6] Even though the sword was replaced by a new one, the current Bohmong referred to the sword as if it was one sword with a continuous history that lives on in the photos that were curated by him.

The current sword is kept in a beautifully engraved box and stored in a secret place within the king's palace. It is worn only during ceremonial events such as the tax collection ceremony or other official state ceremonies.

Figure 14 Bohmongs with ceremonial sword. First image reproduced with permission from Shai Shing Aung.

Bohmong sword and the invention of a Marma tradition

The kingly blade and the symbolic power that it holds is another entry point into the community's history. As seen from the above description, the current Bohmong recounts how the sword connects his current position as ruler to that of the earliest Bohmong. Since the sword is mentioned at the beginning of the group's history as a prize from the powerful King of Arakan, the sword seems to incarnate the legendary rise of the Bohmong within the legend of the migration of a group of people, as well as providing physical evidence of that narrative. Moreover, the sword's linkage with lineage and roots in Pegu seems to add a mythical quality to the object as it reinstates the original Bohmong, the vanquished Prince of Pegu, to his former kingly power.

Even though the version of the sword that can be seen in the photographs was a relatively recent replacement of the original sword, its addition to the ceremonial wardrobe seems to continue the link with an ancestral heritage, connecting the present with different moments in the history of the royal family and affirming the close relationship of the Bohmong with the rulers of Burma, Arakan, and the British Empire. These links are important as they legitimate each new leader as the ruler of this migrating community. Later, in the 1990s, the Bohmong sword converged with another cultural asset, the royal family genogram, and together they became the main objects of veneration, remembrance, and validation of the royal family.

The more recent rendition of the sword seems to carry the same shininess or power of the old and original sword provided by the Arakan king. This adjusted schema is not unlike the analysis of traditional societies on the windward part of Hawaii (Handler and Linnekin, 1984, p. 284) and the use of "Lomi" salmon. Lomi salmon is a surrogate for the kiumu fish.[7] Very few modern Hawaiians are aware that the salmon has replaced the kiumu fish, as for Hawaiians today this historical relationship is irrelevant since the lomi salmon has become just as traditional and meaningful. Through this example, Handler and Linnekin are showing that these adapted customs have as much force and as much meaning for their modern practitioners as other cultural artefacts that can be traced directly to the past. Moreover, the example shows how the re-invention of a tradition in the present is able to continue the link with the past.

The Bohmong sword as symbol of military power

Although it does not seem possible that the Bohmongs of the twentieth century would have been directly involved in battle, it is likely that the early rendition of the sword was a battle-ready sword, not just a symbol of military prowess. In fact the sword represents victory over the various enemies during the group's migration: the military bravery in the face of Portuguese and Mughal invaders and military campaigns against the hostile tribes of the CHT. Moreover, the "shininess" of the Bohmong sword signifies a transformation from defeat of the royal family in Pegu to the success of military campaigns during the migration. The fact that the sword was sanctioned both by the Kings of Arakan and then later by the British Empire points to an object that embodies the military achievements of the Bohmong but also their right to lead the migrating group. The resources such as the sword further help the royal family to establish its authority in the new lands, and are deployed in various ceremonies and scenarios, as the sword bolsters the exemplariness of the centre, making "the realm" more real and powerful.

The tax collection ceremony – the *raj punya*

The Bohmong Circle has maintained the impression of an independent native state with "exceptional status" that was codified in the CHT Regulation of 1900 and sanctioned by an external power – the British – in order to facilitate a more efficient system of tax collection. The political structure of circle chief, headman (leader of district or *mouza*), and *karbari* (village leader) was embodied in the Act of 1900 and then later in the Peace Accord of 1997.

It is also reaffirmed annually in the tax collection ceremony.

The tax collection ceremony used to be held in all three circles; however, now only the Bohmong Circle continues the re-enactment. Local anthropologist Barua in 2001 pointed out the reason why the ceremony was discontinued in the Mong and Chakma Circles:

> In the past such ceremonies were also held in the Mong and Chakma circles for the collection of jum tax. But rajpunna is not being held nowadays in these circles due to deterioration of law and order situation caused by the threat from the insurgents.
>
> (Barua, 2001, p. 42)

When it is held

The tax collection ceremony in the Bohmong Circle, called the *raj punya*, is held between December and January every year. This event is not only a ceremonial collection of tax from the rural parts of the Bohmong Circle, moving through the hierarchies of leadership to the apex. It is also a fair or carnival in which thousands of tribal people take part and pay respect to their chief. The festival, according to my informants, has been re-enacted annually since 1875 – at the time of the 9th Bohmong when British officials intervened in the royal family succession rules (see Figure 15). There are no details about the first recorded *raj punya*, but Lewin in the 1870s mentions a three-day carnival in the hill tracts:

> I had not seen one drunken man nor witnessed any discourtesy to a woman. They seemed an honest kindly people, happy in their homes and in their simple Buddhist faith.
>
> (Lewin, 1885, p. 223)

Who attends

According to the Bohmong, the *raj punya* is the biggest and most colourful traditional festival of the Bohmong Circle. The festival is held in Bandarban and requires the compulsory attendance of headmen, *kabari*, and representatives of all tribes from the Bandarban district. The annual re-enactment follows these steps. All groups – whether Marma or non-Marma – travel across the circle to Bandarban town. The groups include not only the Marma but also the Chakma, Tangchangya, Tripura, Mro, Khumi, Pankhua, Lusai, Khyang, Bawm, and Chak communities. All tribal cultures come to celebrate the re-enactment of tax collection but also their own cultural contribution to the region. The event is held at the *rajbari* compound – the kings' residence in the Hotel Sangu – to celebrate the festival. The "troops" give the Bohmong and his VIP guests a guard of honour when entering the *darbar*

Figure 15 *Raj punya* across time. Reproduced with permission from Shai Shing Aung and Jerry Allen.

(hall) of the royal palace. Young Marma boys and girls greet the king, showering petals on him and performing traditional cultural dances.

Local public representatives, foreign guests, and top government officials in the police and army are present at the function and sit alongside the Bohmong (see Figure 16). On the opening day, *jhum*

Figure 16 *Raj punya* with local representatives – 15th Bohmong: the *raj punya* starts with this formal event. The Raja (who was in his 90s) was escorted to the stage and the people of power in the area (the government representatives, the army, the hill district council, and the district commissioner) were positioned around him. The front rows of the audience were occupied by the institutions of power. The indigenous people stood around the edges. Reproduced with permission from Jerry Allen.

farmers from all over the Bohmong Circle hand over their annual *jhum* tax to their respective headmen and *karbaris*, who formally hand over the money to the king. The Bohmong receives this tax and hands it over to local representatives of the nation state (see Figure 17). The office of the deputy commissioner – originally British and now Bangladeshi – receives 21 per cent from *jhum* cultivation, the headman 37 per cent, and the Bohmong office 42 per cent.

Figure 17 *Raj punya* tax collection: after the speeches, the money, chickens, and bottles of arrack are collected on a table on the side of the stage. Reproduced with permission from Jerry Allen.

After the tax is collected, a variety of ethnic communities perform their culturally unique dances: see Figure 18, the stick dance of the Bawm and the pipes of the Mro.

The *raj punya* is therefore a regional ceremony with all tribes in attendance and the ceremony is led by the Marma leaders, who follow the rules and processes of *jhum* tax collection as defined in the Act of 1900!

Reinventing the tradition

In the Marma case, there is a pre-existing social structure within the hybrid group headed by the Bohmong. This structure is then replicated and endorsed within the context of the British circle

Figure 18 Entertainment at *raj punya*. Reproduced with permission from Jerry Allen.

system, which has the effect of hybridising and expanding the tradition of tax collection.

According to Hobsbawm and Ranger, longstanding traditions are eternally unchanged. But oftentimes traditions once invented can be reinvented. In the case of the Marma, there is a reinterpretation of a longstanding tradition, although the tax collection ceremony in many ways is a replaying of the subjugation of the Marma royal family to the British and to the subsequent powers in the region. It appears that the ceremony has been reinterpreted as an annual re-enactment of a founding event in which the structures of the circle are reaffirmed. This strengthens the cultural content from within and on the boundaries of the Marma group. Moreover, through this manifestation of strength, the ceremony seems to convert a sense of defeat and subjugation to a foreign power, into a narrative of renewed power and triumph.

The connecting power of shininess

The *raj punya* brings different groups together to commemorate this ritual, and this provides the opportunity to display the "shininess" of the Bohmong and the well-being of the circle. During the festival, kingly regalia – golden horns, gongs, spears, parasols, and swords of the faithful followers – are on display, as well as all the photographs of past Bohmongs. The *raj punya* re-enacts the old hierarchy of the power of king, courtiers, and their combined regalia to underlie the authority of the royal layer of Marma society to not only lead the Marma group but the whole circle and other sections of the population living in the rural areas of the circle.

The *raj punya* is therefore a tradition that in many ways was developed because of an encounter with the British, which took the existing tributary system to another level. It imposes fixed practices such as repetition to make sure that the cultural content expressed in the event is reproduced over time. Through the commemorative practices of the annual tax collection ceremony, the community are reminded of the early British interventions in the region when the circle of chiefs was first set up. However, through the display of regalia and pomp, the group are also able to link the ceremony to their origins in Burma. Thus, this reinterpretation of a tradition helps the group to maintain social cohesion and display power, which in turn bolsters the society on its Barthian boundaries with "the other". Moreover, since this "tribe" is institutionalised as a political identity – as a unit of representation with rights, land, and local leaders – the maintenance and reinforcement of that identity becomes important to most of its members.

The coin garlands – *Puaitha Loing Hrui*

Coin garlands,[8] as part of Marma material culture, both symbolically and financially convey a sense of protection for brides.

The custom of coin garland-making

In rural areas of the Bohmong Circle, there is a custom of coin garland-making. Mostly the men of the family would collect the coins from markets and private sellers, and when there were enough coins, a garland of coins would be made. The garlands are typically made up of Indian rupee coins, threaded on a string or on a small chain (see Figure 19). Sometimes there are plastic beads between the coins or white metal beads made from melted-down local coins. I was informed that the garland designs are Burmese in origin but that the garland-makers had to rely on local Bengali smelting techniques and craftsmanship as well as local materials such as plastic beads and chains.

Function of coin garlands

The garlands would be employed as a bride price or bride wealth that would be taken to a marriage table by the bridegroom. Once married, the wives would wear their garlands all day, while working and sleeping, carrying their "personal value" with them.

> She used to wear her necklace outside, because it is made for showing its beauty and preciousness.
>
> (Interview Sathowing Aung, coin garland that was 100 years old)

Wearing the garland also kept them safe, as there was no way of keeping valuables secure in their remote bamboo homes.

Nowadays, the practice of making coin garlands is disappearing, as there are fewer collectable coins on the market. Also, coin garlands have been converted from bride wealth into heirlooms, which are mostly handed down to daughters in the families, with the main function of protecting them from poverty, and the garlands are only worn on special occasions or at Marma cultural events. If not in use, the garlands are dismantled and squirreled away or buried like treasure in the lands surrounding a bamboo home, protecting the coins from theft. Many of the coin garlands have been purchased by the Tribal Cultural Institute in Bandarban and put on display. The coin garlands on show were made from Indian rupee coins with the heads of Queen Victoria, Edward VII, and George V, and post partition of India, there were East Pakistan taka coins depicting George VI.[9] The coin garlands therefore reflect the chequered history of the region.[10]

The coin garlands not only play an instrumental role in cementing marriages and protecting women after marriage,

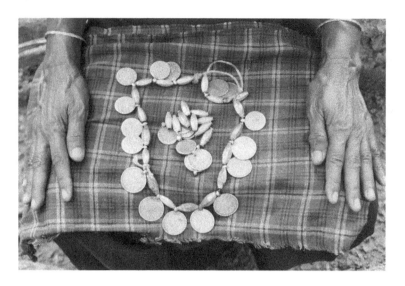

Figure 19 A coin garland.

but they are also symbolic of many themes in the region that convey value and power. The coin garland displays the bride's prestige in terms of "shininess" and this comes from the ongoing connection with the past powers of external, distant kings. Owners of the coin garlands interviewed during the fieldwork claimed that the British kings and queens on the coins are the most powerful rulers. Therefore the garlands seem to convey a kingly cosmic sacred power which linked the rural communities to the "Empire of everywhere". Moreover, the coins symbolically represent royalty, durability, and brilliance, allowing all who wear them to be ritually connected to the same shininess of the rulers that lived beyond the boundaries of the CHT. Therefore, the value of the coin garland is not only monetary but also symbolic of the shininess and radiance of the universal kings, which seems to promise further protection by linking the community of the isolated hill tracts to a place beyond the borderlands.

It was really valuable and expensive at that time. The oldest coin is 170 years old. Even if you want the silver, it costs a lot. You can make a new one but you can't find like this original one.

(Interview Sathowing Aung)

The weight of the silver coins also has monetary value,[11] as many of the garlands have been lost or plundered during the military occupation of the CHT. Therefore, the garlands have become rare and, as a result, even more prized. And finally, the mix of Burmese aesthetics and Bengali craftmanship connect this object to the past and present realities of the community, pointing to a sense of continuity and adaptation.

The function of Marma material culture and ceremonials

Marma material culture has synthesised elements of key historical events while making adjustments to existing schemas, whether two swords serving as one, or the existing hierarchy of the hybrid group becoming part of the British-instigated Bohmong Circle, or when the coin garlands incorporate elements of Bengali craftmanship to continue the Burmese cultural practice of bride wealth. There is a change in form, but the material culture and ceremonies still seem to convey an unchanging essence and, despite the discontinuities in material form, the present continues to incarnate past realities. Through the processes of creation and maintenance, the objects and ceremonies also bring together the hybrid groups as one ethnic identity. To understand the nature of the processes that have instilled singularity in meaning through

Marma material culture, the next sections will examine the three objects and ceremonies from different theoretical perspectives.

Invention and reinvention

The group is far away from the centre, busy developing a new centre, and is aided in this endeavour through the invention of material culture and ceremony. It seems that there is a sense of Marma histories being re-invented and reproduced through the sword, the tax collection ceremony, and the coin garland. The traditions and form of the objects and ceremonies undergo some adaptions over time, which help the invented traditions to continue to act as a link with a historic past (Hobsbawm and Ranger, 2012). With the lens of invented traditions, we can also see that the sword, which was gifted from different external kings, carries the shininess and power of those kings. This shininess was borrowed for different purposes, whether to enhance the authority of the Bohmong who wears the sword or in the kingly regalia at the *raj punya* that gives the king authority over different communities in the circle of power. The annual re-enactment of the tax collection ceremony, although it represents a subjugation to first the British Empire and then the state of Bangladesh, is reinterpreted today as an opportunity to display radiance and power, which helps to bolster the apex and therefore helps towards legitimising Bohmong authority. The effect of invention of material culture and re-enactment of ceremonies is that it reproduces a cultural identity that signals radiance and triumph, which in turn cements the group and helps it to manifest a singular identity in the region.

Entanglement

There are some common elements to the three examples of Marma material culture which point to processes at work as part of the hybrid group's move to singularity. The sword, the annual re-enactment of the subjugation of the group to first the British and then the nation state, and the coins with British rulers point to Marma material culture and ceremonies as entangled objects and ceremonies. For example, Thomas describes the effects of entanglement on a culture which seem relevant to the Marma:

> In some areas, entanglement with colonizing agents of various kinds has gone on for hundreds of years and has prompted a distinctive indigenous historical consciousness in which local customs and solidarity are explicitly contrasted with the inequality characteristic of relations with outsiders. But such contacts are not only historically crucial – they also energize a new way of thinking about material culture.
>
> (Thomas, 1991, p. 4)

The Bohmong's power is in itself already foreign, originating from Pegu and deriving its new power from Arakan. Thus, where other ethnic groups have entered into subordinate relations with the Bohmong, they are also subordinating themselves collectively to this shiny powerful foreignness, unifying different groups to be ruled by the same power. The group was gifted the sword, power was given to circle chiefs, and coins were introduced to the region as it became part of a wider state and then a global economy. These objects and ways of collecting tax originated from foreign kings and empires. At first, the group became part of a gift economy as it embodied the characteristics of the donor, which embedded the group in relations of indebtedness and reciprocity. However, over time, the objects and ceremonies became incorporated within the framework of local meanings as foreign things or "entangled objects" as actors incorporated some of the values of the objects and rejected others as the group shaped their own singularly entangled history.

Sahlins also contributes to a sense of continuity and singularity of essence when he discusses the incorporation or grafting of new elements onto old core ones as part of the reproduction of structure. For example, shininess is similar to *mana* as the appropriation of Cook's bones leads to the *mana* of Hawaiian kingship becoming British and this entangled nature of *mana* is reinforced by objects such as swords that were gifted by the British to Sahlins' islanders.[12]

> [M]ana is the creative power Hawaiians describe as making visible what is invisible, causing things to be seen, which is the same as making them known or giving them form. Hence the divine of chiefs is manifest in their brilliance, their shining.
>
> (Sahlins, 1981, p. 31)

Both the sword and the coin garland have a metallic quality, conveying a sense of shininess, brilliance, and radiance, which also quite likely alludes to the kingship's eternity. Moreover, the amplification of the elements of shininess in all the royal bodies and objects acts as the cement between the hybrid subgroups of Bohmong families and followers, while at the same time radiating a single essence of the group.

Syncretism

Another important aspect is the process behind the Marma's synthesis of these objects, which are foreign yet merged with Burmese practice to create a sense of continuity with Pegu and Burma. As with Herskovits' syncretism, these elements of culture from a past also offer a mode of uniting the past with the present. Additionally, when there is nothing familiar in the new context, cultural traits that are more dominant are carried over into new cultural contexts and reinterpreted in light of their new surroundings. The coin garland, the sword, and the hierarchy of the tax collection ceremony are survivals from the past, adapted to the new environment and updated. Moreover, Herskovits saw the importance of the journey of an ethnic group as contributing to this process. For example, with Marma material culture, the further the group moved away from Burma, and to its new home, the more it held onto certain elements of Burmese culture such as shininess, garland-making, and the hierarchy of power, and these were maintained and elaborated upon while other elements fell away.

Final thoughts on migration, settlement, and material culture

We have learnt that while the Marma group have absorbed many cultural elements from their wider environment, they regularly turn inwards towards the ritualised apex of the Bohmong. The emphasis on links with Burma and the symbolic power of material culture inform a culturally grounded action strategy that legitimates their right to rule. Traditional rituals have been reproduced as old structures in a new setting, with new elements absorbed along the way. Even if the rituals have been adapted or invented afresh, the Marma still perceive them as essential embodiments. Thus, the sword embodies continuity of power, the *raj punya* continuity in re-enactment, and the coin garland continuity through adaptation. All three embody "shininess" as the objects and practices travelled with the group from the land in the East where the sun rises, adding a further layer of enchantment to the narratives.

The chapters on migration and material culture have illustrated the value of examining the community in the *longue durée*. You can see the reproduction of structure plotted on a historical timeline, the cyclical nature of events, and the moment when structures reach a point of collapse as illustrated by the photo of the destroyed *rajbari* (Figure 12). The narratives around the material objects also move on the historical timeline, but, in contrast to the migration narratives, the stories are created in the present to help maintain the link with the past.

The Marma royal family have become a multi-family dynasty. However, the succession rules have also resulted in the overstretching of the system of the royal family and land ownership – and this is evoked in the photo of the *rajbari* and its loss to the community. More significantly, the photo symbolises the royal family's waning of power in the region as well as the opening of the boundaries of the town to outsiders. Even against the backdrop of the uncertain future centred around the loss of land, the royal family of the Marma community still have a clear narrative of where they come from and what makes them different compared to other communities in the area.

The chapters on migration, settlement, and material culture have illustrated Marma intentionality and purposefulness in creating a group identity and anchoring it in a locality. Marma identity is lived passionately to this day.

Conclusions

This is a study of a remarkable group of people who inhabit the militarised borderlands of Bangladesh. My first impression of the Marma people was that they were a migrating clan, marooned on the CHT. They had survived various waves of change, unchanged. However, during the process of putting this study together, I came to appreciate much more about Marma society, history, and identity.

The key finding of this study is that an ethnically heterogenous migrating group from Burma evolved during migration (and after) into an ethnically homogenous community that came to identify itself as Marma. Subsequently, parts of this community's rituals change or are re-invented, but their immanent order is persistent over time and this persistence forms the basis for an equally persistent sense of Marma-ness. The book has illustrated the importance of examining everyday rituals and systems in historical context in order to understand the resilience and creativity of an ethnic group like the Marma, as well as the importance of bringing to bear an array of anthropological theories – rather than a single theory – to understand the various processes at work in the creation of Marma identity.

During the recurrent themes of exile, migration, settlement, conflict, and travelling through unfamiliar terrain, the leading noble class encountered diversity, difference, and entanglement. This royal layer incorporated the many cultural shards and influences to become ethnically plural. Over time, these elements merged into one ethnic whole as the group came to identify as Marma.

The journey on the migration path triggered processes of selecting the cultural traits and embarking on a self-making ethnicity project:

1. syncretically, as the migrating community moved away from Burma to new lands and then back in the direction of Burma as they settled in the CHT;
2. through the rituals that protected the new settlement in the CHT;
3. through tightening marriage customs and reproducing marriage rituals; and
4. through incorporating foreign artefacts of material culture that ultimately became Marma.

In all of the above processes, the selection or ordering of key characteristics of the ethnically hybrid group not only pushed its members to regularly define itself in terms of a singular identity with links to Burma, but also demonstrated the community's ability to respond to new environments and encounters with new peoples. As a result, no matter how far from Burma the migrating group that became Marma travelled, it retained a sense of a Burmese origin.

Even with this history of significant ethnic hybridity, the book has illuminated some of the processes which continuously reproduce a core of relations and practices that are unique to the Marma and which have survived change. In various chapters, the study details the core practices and relations that continue to reiterate and emphasise the original link with Burma, from naming practices, marriage rituals, elopement, inheritance laws that include Marma women, and the *oeingsa* household compound to shiny swords of state, coin garlands, ceremonies, and royal palaces. In fact, it appears that the persistent staging of "traditional" Marma customs, structures, rituals, and material culture reflect the Marma senses of a "substantive content" (Shils, 1981, p. 263) and unchanging essence, as Marma culture responds to changes in the external environment. Moreover, the book illustrates that Marma material culture and ceremony is organised and assembled in relation to its history and synthesised to stress a coherent and continuous connection with Burmese and Arakanese times, again building on core practices.

The continuous encounters with forces outside the community have pushed the Marma to differentiate themselves through inventions and inversions of tradition, and material culture. Indeed, whether in relation to the royal chart or the tax collection ceremony – the *raj punya* – the Marma people have made use of entanglement and material culture to strengthen the ethnic group's cultural essence and at the heart of these inventions is the distillation of "shininess". At the beginning, before migration, we learn about the radiance of swords and white elephants and gold. At the end, on arriving in the CHT, the Marma as a settled community display the shininess of the kingly blade, coin garlands, and golden temples, all of which signify that a continuity is achieved through a core of "shininess". Thus, the processes of discontinuity and continuity through cultural invention and inversion add to the impression of a distinct culture responding to various kinds of imposed and voluntary change.

Finally, an important insight in the study is how Marma people work towards protecting Marma identity from blending and mixing with Bengali outsiders, which otherwise could result in the loss of Marma lands to outsiders and therefore potentially halt the cultural reproduction of Marma identity. Interestingly, whereas the Burmese reaction to intermarriage focusses mostly on the fears around the dilution of Buddhist culture, in Chapter 5 I show that Marma fears revolve around the loss of land through marriage. Scott's theories help to makes sense of the Marma conundrum of out-marriage to non-Buddhists. Through this lens, it can be shown that out-marriage would not only mean the loss of the gift of land to a non-Buddhist but also a potential future blending of identities through the children. Therefore, Marma girls are the potential point of weakness for maintaining ethnic endogamy, and, consequently, steps are taken through strict marriage rules, taboos, customary law, and the threat of ostracisation to block Marma women's marriage with Bengalis. This has also informed recent moves towards suppressing the ethnic diversity of the group while allowing some flexibility in practice, for example by including Bengali dowries in Marma marriage customs to encourage traditional Marma marriages to take place. Even with the flexibility in customs and practice, the overall endogamy rules on the boundaries of culture are adhered to. However, despite living in close symbiosis with the state, intermarriage with the majority population remains to this day a huge anxiety for the Marma community and this is heightened by the continuing changes in the demographics of the CHT in favour of Bengalis and the growing impingement on land ownership.

These key points postulate that the Marma group, operating from its hybridity, undergoes internal reconfigurations that help move the community towards a singular identity and, at the same time, a core set of practices are continuously adapted to change in order to be reproduced. While the process of restricted hybridisation through marriage rules reduces the force of socio-cultural differences that build up within the Marma realm, there is an immanent drive to define its core characteristics in terms of a connection with Burma. Thus, while the subgroups within the Marma community are mixed and culturally borrowing from each other, it is possible to see a structural core of cultural memory, practice, and identity being reproduced as an active ordering force in Marma lives. The book has therefore demonstrated that Marma identity is multi-layered, able to adapt and transform structures at the point of collapse. But is also essentially stable amid manifest flux and change.

How does the book contribute to existing debates in anthropology on ethnic identity on the borderlands? It underlies the importance of applying different perspectives on identity on borderlands. The approaches of hybridity, creolisation and syncretism alone do not adequately address how identity processes respond to change over time. By analysing cultural hybridity in the historical *long durée* – a combination of theories with a historical perspective – we can see entanglement and syncretism at work over time, and an essential Marma cultural core in action. Moreover, the book illustrates the importance of studying hill societies – their history, location, their residence patterns, their kinship practices, their customs and rituals, and to see them as largely social and historical choices designed to position themselves vis a vis the valley states and other hill peoples among whom they live.

The book also reveals the limitations of some of the theories. Scott's case studies on cultural entanglement and hybridity as "the universal condition of chaos" (Scott, 2005, p. 213) are initially relevant to the Marma setting. The leaders of the Marma migrating group, in a semantically empty land, build boundaries through shrines. Through this process, the group become less of an amalgam of cultures and more singular, especially when deciding who would be protected within the shrine boundaries. However, the findings of this study also show that theories can become quickly irrelevant as the conditions change. For example, Scott's theory does not help navigate situations where geographic boundary-making is eroded with the influx of new populations. And the maintenance of the shrine boundaries through the Bandarban edict, which makes it a taboo for Marma individuals to die outside the boundaries, has increased maternal mortality, placing the Marma population at further risk. In this recent context, the Marma ethnic group has shifted from boundary-making to openly articulating their identity through objects and rituals, and constructing new Buddhist temples, to convince others in the region of Marma rootedness to the land. Thus, first boundaries and the creation of sacred sites was a response to settlement of empty land. The encroachment of this land has triggered new ways of maintaining the singularity of Marma identity and shown the usefulness of employing a different set of theories to help examine this process.

With hybridity theories, there is little insight into who or which group of people makes the selections of characteristics that move it to a singular identity. To illuminate these processes, this study has contributed to the anthropological studies of *agency* in the context of processes of cultural continuity and change. The book explored the agency of the members of the royal family as they mediate between the changing states and "society", vernacularising ideals and adapting them to the local, as in the case of the tax collection ceremony. The study surveyed the historical narratives that provide a shared sense of history to the society, also as a form of agency, whether as written accounts by royal historians such as U Tan Pru; visualised in the royal chart by Maung Nue Sein, the director of the Tribal Cultural Institute; or the published accounts of colonial visitors to the region, for example Hutchinson (1906) and Mills (1927), who are often cited by recent Marma historians. And finally, the analysis highlighted the agency of marriage ritual experts in transmitting their knowledge of the rituals from one generation to another, as well as the role of the *medechar* in practising and interpretating the rituals during marriage, thereby upholding the traditional core of Marma identity. In short, the analysis has shown how agency has helped to bolster Marma claims to land and legitimate their existence in the area, as well to manufacture a mythical nature to Marma-ness (Trevor-Roper, 2008).

Do the Marma people experience or understand their history in the same way as outlined in the book? The answer to this question would require further research! The ritual marriage experts and *medechar*, who have an age-long task and responsibility to reproduce cultural processes, would agree with the findings in this thesis. The royal family are actively inventing and reinventing tradition. In doing so, they are adapting culture and tradition to continue its practice. And those who work closely with the Tribal Cultural Institute with the remit to conserve and promote culture may be cognisant of these processes, but whether the actors are aware that they are the agents of a Marma identity process is not clear. To get to the bottom of this, being an observer during the regular meetings of the counsel of princes would deepen the understanding of the workings of the royal family but also establish whether there is an awareness of the maintenance of a core set of practices and "shininess".

The research in this book has shown that an interpretation of cultural life on the peripheries of a state cannot be deduced from traditional state classifications of hill peoples. On the contrary, the CHT borderlands are highly complex and therefore need to be studied from the bottom up, taking into account multiple perspectives, the agency of actors on the ground, and narratives surrounding the origin and purposing of iconic material culture. Only this way can we get close to understanding the lived experience of an ethnic community in such remote and complex zones of the world.

For much of its history, the CHT in Zomia was unique in being the only non-Islamic, non-Bengali, non-wet-rice-growing, and low-population-density district in an overwhelmingly Muslim Bengali nation state. With the liberation of Bangladesh from East Pakistan in 1971, sweeping and unwelcome changes to the CHT were set into motion. It heralded an era in which the CHT region became increasingly administered by the state. Even in name the new "Bangla Desh", translating loosely as "land of the Bangla", was an openly mono-ethnic nation that would not easily tolerate multi-ethnicity and any resistance to Bengali norms in the CHT. For some time, there has been a government-sponsored Bengali in-migration into the CHT, but, significantly, for the next census of 2021, the ethnic categories of the CHT have been removed altogether. Whereas before assimilation was a choice, now cultural homogenisation seems to be an inevitability. This is particularly relevant at a time when on the other side of the border – in Myanmar – the nation state is making a similar stand on ethno-religious differences. In 2017, fears around hybridity, entanglement, and the mixing of cultures saw a period of unprecedented violence, which resulted in the expulsion of the Muslim Rohingya community from Myanmar. On the CHT side, something in reverse seems to be happening. As the study has illustrated, one Buddhist minority under pressure to assimilate is instead increasing its numbers and sharpening its identity. There are stricter marriage rules to maintain access to land, there is an acceleration of the building of Buddhist temples, more males are becoming Buddhist monks, and there is an intensification of ritual life. In view of these fascinating and diverse reactions to change on the borderlands, a study of one very distinct ethnic group in this region serves not only as an important marker of ethnic determinism, but also hopefully as a celebration of difference within Bangladesh and beyond.

Notes

Introduction

1. A bloody secessionist struggle against dominant West Pakistan, which was fought along ethnic and linguistic lines, costing three million lives.
2. I will be using the term *Arakan* often. *Arakan* was an independent kingdom for most of its history. It was also ruled by Indian kingdoms and Burmese Empires. Today, the territory forms the Rakhine State in Myanmar.
3. In this book, I will be using the term "Bengali" in reference to language and sometimes ethnicity, and Bangladeshi to denote citizenship of Bangladesh.
4. Sheikh Hasina Wazed is the current prime minister of Bangladesh and she has been in office since January 2009.
5. There are two Marma words to describe shininess: "taukte" and "lanre", with an additional "al" to mean strength or power. "Alan raung" can cover both shininess and power. The root of these Marma words is connected with Rakhine or Burmese language.
6. Land scarcity and ownership has long been an important topic in this region, but due to military control of the CHT it is impossible to research this sensitive topic in any detail.
7. Many royal family members moved "back" to Myanmar during the Independence War of the 1970s, and now in response to the influx of Bangladeshis into the region.
8. In order to stay in Bandarban, I needed permission from the local power structures such as the Bohmong *Raja* and the district commissioner. I presented a letter from University College London and from the Horniman museum in London,

detailing my objectives for the research and requesting that the Tribal Cultural Institute of Bandarban assist with my work.

9. In 1991, an independent fact-finding commission – the Chittagong Hill Tracts Commission – described the CHT as "a military occupied area. The military dominates all spheres of life." As a counter-insurgency measure, there is a large number of armed personnel in the Hill Tracts, and the human rights violations in the area have been attributed in large measure to their continuing presence. In 1980, an estimated 30,000 regular and paramilitary troops were stationed in the hill tracts and the number of police stations doubled in the four years from 1976 to 1980. Inevitably, the presence of the armed forces in such large numbers has provoked conflicts and tribal people feel intimidated by the armed presence.

10. "People are busy looking back and feeling the pain and trauma of the 1971 War of Independence. The Shabag movement is an example of this – a lenient verdict on a war criminal from 40 years ago sparks off a revolution in Shabag square in Dhaka. It spreads to the CHT. The country is still dealing with its past and not getting on with the problems of now." (Fieldnotes 12 December 2013 – Butcher of Mirapur, or Abdul Quader Mullah, is hanged in Dhaka.)

2 The project and the people

1. Chittagonian is Bengali with a strong local dialect.
2. In 1795 Francis Buchanan was attached to the embassy at Ava, the capital of Burma, as a medical doctor.
3. Thomas Herbert Lewin (1839–1919). In 1857, Lewin travelled to India as a lieutenant and was involved in several campaigns to put down the Indian Mutiny. He became a district police superintendent in Chittagong in October 1864. In March 1866, he was promoted to captain. His appointment, first as temporary superintendent and later as permanent deputy commissioner and political agent for the unregulated hill tracts – a post that he held until 1875 – meant that he became in effect the governor of the remote Lushai and CHT. Based

on his experiences, he wrote *The Hill Tracts of Chittagong and the Dwellers therein* (Calcutta, 1869), *The Wild Races of South-Eastern India* (England, 1870), *Hill Proverbs of the Inhabitants of the Chittagong Hill Tracts* (1873), and *A Fly on the Wheel* (1885).

4. Robert Henry Sneyd Hutchinson (1866–1930). In 1905, he was district superintendent in the Bengal Police Department. In 1906, he published *An Account of the Chittagong Hill Tracts*.

5. J. P. Mills (1890–1960). Mills joined the Indian Civil Service in 1913 and was posted to Assam Province where he became well known for his monographs on the Nagas.

6. Emil Riebeck (1853–1885) was a German explorer, mineralogist, ethnologist, and naturalist. He travelled to the CHT with the ethnographer Adolf Bastian in 1882.

7. Arakan was an independent kingdom for most of its history. It was also ruled by Indian kingdoms and Burmese Empires. Today, the territory forms the Rakhine State in Myanmar.

8. The East India Company (also the English East India Company, and sometimes the British East India Company) was incorporated by royal charter in 1600 as an English joint-stock company formed for the exploitation of trade with East and Southeast Asia and India.

9. The appointment of a "Superintendent of Hill Tribes" was ostensibly "to administer justice to the Hill people in our jurisdiction, and to prevent that oppression and plunder of poor and ignorant savages by the crafty Bengallee moneylender which may lead, as in the case of the Sonthals, to violence and bloodshed" (Government of Bengal, Judicial Proceedings 142-3, December 1862).

10. According to Lewin (1885, p. 123), "Karna-phuli" means an "ear-flower" or "ear-ring". The story comes from the Mughal period, when the wife of the governor dropped her valuable earring in a river and was drowned trying to retrieve it. The local name of the river is Kynsa-khyoung.

11. The notion "non-hill man resident" is a new conception in relation to land settlement in the CHT. Since this provision,

influential non-resident Bengalis can now easily apply for land leased directly to the district commissioner.

12. Since the Second World War, Zomia has experienced a massive transfer, both planned and spontaneous, of lowland populations to the hills. "There they serve the dual purpose of peopling the frontiers with a presumably loyal population and producing cash crops for export, while relieving population pressure in the valleys. Demographically, it represents a conscious strategy of engulfment and eventual absorption" (Scott, 2009, p. 325).

13. In contrast, during the British phase, Bengali entrepreneurial activity was expected to undermine and compete with the British new territorial system of surplus extraction and also lead to tensions in the hills. Consequently, the colonial authorities acted as the protectors of "tribal" rights in the Chittagong Hills. This regulation temporarily halted the tide of Bengalisation but also isolated the hill people from the rest of Bengal (Van Schendel, 1992, pp. 110–111).

14. My informants often recounted his political slogan "forget your tribal identity, be Bengali" to illustrate how his leadership increased anxieties in the hill tracts.

15. According to Gellner and Schendel, an army presence on the frontiers can take the form of nation-state patriotism to counterbalance any cultural loyalties to the nation across the border (Gellner and Schendel, 2013, p. 18).

3 A toolkit to study identity on the borderlands: a brief summary

1. In which time is *durée* or duration.

4 Marma kinship and marriage rituals

1. The members of the homestead, bound together by common interests and sentiment, pay loyalty to the *bari* head as a manifestation of unity and cohesion.

2. Another common belief is that a marriage between family members may ease the transition for the bride and ensure a more caring attitude from her in-laws, leading to greater marital stability.
3. The data presented in Shenk et al. (2016) suggest that consanguineous marriage decisions are often strategic. For example, a daughter with no brothers might marry a cousin to retain rights to family property, or a family might choose to marry an educated daughter to an unrelated spouse in order to "make new relatives".
4. This group includes Bunjogis, Pankhos, Mros, Tipras (Lewin, 1884, p. 227).
5. This was a traditional home, but with internet and skype to stay in touch with family members abroad.
6. While these shared rituals helped to create a sense of unity as they worked together to thank the eldest brother for heading the compound, they were divided when it came to which *kyang* to worship at. One household followed a monk called Guru Bante and went to his private temple, while others worshipped exclusively at the *royal kyang*. This division was a relatively new phenomenon that emerged in the last ten years. Moreover, this household was related to the 14th Bohmong so they had an uneasy relationship with the 15th Bohmong family.
7. For the Marma, the parent–daughter bond is strong, with the youngest daughters often staying with their parents and enjoying land or property while the parents are still alive. Other children inherit after death and sons also inherit substantial property from their wives.
8. Bernot also mentions the centrality of the astrologer in marriage in the Marma community of the 1950s (Bernot, 1967b, p. 180).
9. It seems that Marma people living as a majority in the Bohmong Circle tend to have three names while Marma people in the Mong Circle, as a minority in a mostly Tripura

region, tend to take one name with "Marma" as their family name. The Marmas of Bandarban are closely linked to their Bohmong family and consequently do not need to assert their identity in this way.

10. Astrologers check if couples have a history of mental health. Moreover, according to the elders, 27 birth stars are split into 3 categories: human, spirit, and ogres. Ogres and humans are not a match but all others are.

11. The sword represents the strength and length of a union.

12. They constitute the basic code of ethics to be undertaken by lay followers of Buddhism. The precepts are commitments to abstain from killing living beings, stealing, sexual misconduct, lying, and intoxication.

13. The deputy commissioner and political agent of the unregulated CHT – Thomas Herbert Lewin – wrote about Marma marriage customs in a chapter on the hill tracts dated between 1866 and 1867.

14. The entrails of a fowl were examined, and dreams studied by the female relatives of both parties and interpreted according to a set of rules. An astrologer was consulted for a favourable day for the marriage. Lewin describes the marriage feast as being accompanied by a fiery *arrack* made ready by the dozen and that, on the wedding day, the bridegroom arrives at the bride's village with much number and noise. The bride's relations bar his entrance with crossed bamboos unless he pays a forfeit. During the ceremony, a new spun cotton thread is wound round the man and girl. A spirit priest (not unlike the spirit priest that presided over the house puja in the Introduction chapter) mumbles holy words and feeds rice to the wedded couple (Lewin, 1885, p. 228).

15. Maybe this is why the groom's side gives chickens and seems strongly associated with them. If so, hens and cockerel are signs of fertility because they (may) symbolise (a) beings that are of the sky but have come to ground; and (b) the actual genesis of human sexuality as Marma understand this as not just sexual fertility per se.

16. Chickens and eggs have many uses: in divination, to help find a cure for an illness, and to guide the newly deceased family member's soul to the ancestral lands.
17. Tapp describes a Miao ritual in Sichuan, there is a special supper in the evening of the wedding day, during which the bride's side offer a cockerel and the bridegroom's side present a hen. After they are cooked, divination by chicken tongue – *sua qas nphlaib* – takes place, and if the tongues are not damaged in any way, the signs are considered to be lucky (Tapp, 2003, pp. 272, 300).
18. For the Marma, this is not always the case as the bridegroom can also join the woman's family.
19. Ahern's ethnography in Taiwan on Chinese women's power and pollution (Feng, 2012 p. 15) may shed further light from a different perspective on this particular chicken ritual. Chinese women are considered unclean or polluting because of the nature of the "unclean substances" that are associated with menstrual blood and the blood of a virgin's first intercourse which connects this act to birth.
20. As demonstrated in the following verse of a Miao song: Rongjiang Miao "Chicken-Killing Chant" (Translated by Xianghong Feng)

Chicken

Today we are going to decide a marriage

You are the best witness

We are here not for eating you

Just for settling down our children's marriage. (Feng, 2012, p. 6)

5 Ethnic endogamy: land, culture, and religion

1. The taboo marriages encompass marriages with parallel cousins who are viewed as having the same blood ties as siblings.

2. The Bohmong recounted the story of a husband who lived with a woman for three years but married another. The Bohmong consulted customary law, which draws upon ancient Burmese texts, and made the decision to fine the man 30,000 taka. The man could have gone to prison but instead continues to live with his girlfriend, while his new wife is happy with 30,000 taka. Most importantly, social peace is restored.

3. Rule 52: the special status of the region by underlining that "henceforth the Hill Tracts shall be declared an excluded area".

4. Attitudes to Bangladeshi Muslims can be seen in historical records. Lewin in 1885 states: "The Burman, or Mugh, was a fellow creature, without caste prejudices, with a noble religion, a man with whom I could eat, drink, and make fellowship: the Chittagong Bengali was like a fox with a cross of the cat..." (Lewin, 1885, p. 135).

5. In 1938, there had been an anti-Indian riot which saw intense communal violence in colonial Burma. This had resulted in a 350-page book called *Kabya Pyatthana* (The half-caste problem) by U Pu Galay and covered "the question of the marriage of their womenfolk with foreigners in general and with Indians in particular" and the half-caste children that resulted, which threatened Burmese culture and race (Ikeya, 2013, p. 1). According to Ikeya, this polemic against intermarriage and miscegenation was representative of the 1930s in Burma.

6. Debates about which law was to be applied in interstate succession were not about religious traditions or communal identities but a gendered negotiation over the power and authority to define familial bonds and control over who had access to property and privilege and who did not.

7. Burmese Muslims at this time were known as Pathi or *Zerbadee*, a term which usually denoted someone with a Burmese mother and Muslim father. Now known as "Burmese Muslims", they are linguistically and culturally integrated into Burmese society. Citizens are persons who belong to one

of the national races (Kachin, Kayah (Karenni), Karen, Chin, Burman, Mon, Rakhine, Shan, Kaman, or *Zerbadee*) or whose ancestors settled in the country before 1823, the beginning of British occupation of Arakan State. If a person cannot provide evidence that his ancestors settled before this time, then they are not considered to be citizens. They were considered to be a threat to colonial administrators as mixed marriages are not culturally clear in terms of being difficult to place in a hierarchy – they are unstable and amorphous (Ikeya, 2013).

8. With the recent Rohingya crisis, it is evident that these attitudes remain towards Muslims in Myanmar.

9. Myanmar's Protection of Race and Religion Laws were adopted in 2015. They cover (a) Monogamy Law, which makes it a criminal offence to have more than one spouse; (b) Religious Conversion Law and Interfaith Marriage Law, which regulate the marriages of Buddhist women to non-Buddhist men; and (c) Population Control Law, which imposes on women in certain regions the requirement to space the birth of their children by 36 months apart.

10. She assumed the newly created role of state counsellor, a role akin to a prime minister or a head of government, but is now (2021) in prison.

11. Bride payment is a gift not a loan. It protects women when widowed or divorced and is common in Burmese societies. It is settled on the bride (being gifted into trust) by agreement at the time of the wedding, or as provided by law.

12. Bride wealth is marriage payments from the husband and his kin to the bride's kin. Essentially this means that bride wealth marriages are those in which the groom (and often his family) remit a payment in some form to the bride's family in order to officialise a marriage.

13. A dowry is a sum of money or goods, and it comes from the wife's family to her husband's family. In the Bengali Bangladesh tradition, property or money is brought by a bride to her husband on their marriage.

14. Leach similarly identified the importance of ritual wealth in objects and things as the marker of superiority. Hpaga or "wealth items" are symbolic currency for exchanges like bride price but also a repayment for "violations" of the *mayu-dama* rules, incest taboos, or for the resolution of feuds (Leach, 1970, p. 153).

6 Migration and settlement

1. According to Khan (1999), there are several groups of Maghs based on locality and occupation. For example, Khoungtha Magh and Roang Magh are migrants from Arakan. The Barua Maghs are of mixed origin – Hindu, Muslim, Arakanese, Burmese, Portuguese.
2. Francis Buchanan (1798) is one of the first colonial travellers in the CHT to have met with the leader Kong Hla Hpru who was the 5th Bohmong (1727–1811) and the first Bohmong to live in the Bandarban region.
3. Mills claims that Marma succession is similar to primitive Indonesian customs whereby a minor would be passed over in favour of his uncle, "simply because a minor's hands are feeble, but a capable son of full age would not be so passed over" (Mills, 1927, p. 78).
4. The Hanthawaddy Kingdom was the dominant kingdom that ruled lower Burma (Myanmar) from 1287 to 1539 and from 1550 to 1552.
5. Talaing is considered a branch of the great Tai race from Southern and Central China. They had already begun to migrate south, south-west, and south-east, and filtered through Assam, the Chindwin Valley, and Arakan. "This is the stock from which the Maghs are sprung" (Mills, 1927, p. 74).
6. U Tan Pru left the CHT at the time of Partition. His handwritten notes were left behind with the royal family.
7. Jesse is descended from the 15th King, 27 years old in 2015. Jewel is a descendent of the 13th King.

8. The king of Arakan married the princess and changed her name from Shan Dwang Huaung to Cho Han Gree, which means chief queen.
9. Also Burman, Burmese, and Bamar are a Sino-Tibetan ethnic group and nation native to Myanmar (Burma) where they are the dominant group. The Bamar live primarily in the Irrawaddy River basin and speak the Burmese language, which is the sole official language of Myanmar at a national level. Bamar customs and identity are closely intertwined with the broader Burmese culture.
10. The Mon were originally from Southwest China, from where they migrated to upper Burma reportedly around 1500 BC, and then continued moving south to the Irrawaddy valley where the majority of them live today. The Mon are considered descendants of one of Southeast Asia's most ancient civilisations, and they introduced both written language and Buddhism to Burma.
11. The prince was appointed Governor of Chittagong, or *Sait-Tat-Gong*, which means head Fortress in Arakanese (Pru, 1950, p. 9).
12. Under King Chande Wijaya.
13. For circa 18 years.
14. Places such as Ramu, Edgar, Bongoo, Youngtha, Matamuri, and Lama.
15. In 1825, Bohmongree Thet Than Prue became blind and so Thadaw Tun Hla Prue officiated and renewed the settlement with the British in the year 1826 (Pru, 1950, p. 17).
16. Mills (1927, p. 77) connects the Bohmong with the "Regratsa clan" (Rigiesa).
17. This historic event marked the beginning of British rule in Mizoram that lasted until Indian Independence in 1947. Indirectly, it also paved the way for Christian missionaries to introduce Christianity among the Lushais, who came to be known as Mizos.

18. British practice of rewarding with gifts and titles those who rendered services for their causes. In the Lushai expedition, the Bohmong Chief was honoured with a Burmese title that meant "the Chief who holds the golden title" (Baura, 2019, pp. 32, 46).
19. "The Regray Chaung was tidal and deep then and big boats could come up far" (Pru, 1950, p. 15).
20. "[S]ince ancient times when kings started to rule Bandarban, the river was worshipped by the people here as god. The people of Bandarban believe the river is God and the tradition of worshipping it still goes on today, every year. From very early morning, the people came to the river. All the people from the Marma community came together." A quote from a commoner: Mong of Bangladeshi Idol (2013).
21. ST Prue – Kai's father. The headman's own building was made from a mixture of mud and bricks, so he too needed to take shelter in the palace.
22. However, because of this edict and tradition, people who are seriously ill in Bandarban are refusing to go to hospital, for fear of dying and not being able to return home and have a Buddhist funeral. In fact, local NGOs flagged this edict as being partly responsible for a rise in maternal mortality in the region.
23. Similarly, Ortner's early clan-history of the Sherpa repeatedly mentions the carrying of gold and silver objects, riding horses, and visions directing migration choices (Ortner, 1989, pp. 27–29).

7 The invention of Marma material culture and ceremonials

1. "The whole material culture of the tribes of the Chittagong Hill Tracts, under a superficial layer of Bengali and Buddhist culture, is purely and typically Indonesian. They have the typical Indonesian tension-loom, the typical fire-thong, the typical fish-trap lined with cane-thorns, houses, type of

hearths, traps, method of cultivation, and so on" (Mills, 1927, p. 288).

2. Ralph Fitch, a merchant visiting Pegu at the time of Emperor Shweti, was not only interested in noting commercial opportunities in the various places he visited, but, as with Francis Buchanan's travels (1798), he also included descriptive material about the people he met, their dress, appearance, and any strange and exotic customs.

3. Until recently, when the Burmese military junta re-named it Mahabandoola Park, anyone travelling to Rangoon would have found Fitche [sic] Square, a well-known landmark named in honour of the first Englishman to reach Burma.

4. "Luck, everybody cannot become king due to being eldest and fittest, so before me 20 candidates died. I crossed 20 members. But I became king anyway." 17th Bohmong interview.

5. According to a local historian, the 9th Bohmong was honoured with a cross chain at the time of the Lusai expedition and when Queen Victoria was Empress of India. The group was also given 160 musket rifles. The local historian believes that the sword of the Bohmong was stolen during Partition and is now in a Delhi museum.

6. Given the migration history of this descent group, it was interesting how the sword had come to symbolise kingly power, even though there is no coronation (no crown) but instead a handing down of a sword at an installation ceremony sanctioned by the Bangladeshi government. The sword's history is mostly unknown in this Marma family. The first reference to the Bohmong sword can be found in literature when Francis Buchanan recounts Kong H. Prue's (5th Bohmong) narrative on Marma naming and the sword (Buchanan, 1798). However, the theme continues as another type of sword is given to the approximately 95 headmen who run the smaller districts in the province for the Bohmong. Moreover, I observed that the *dao* sword was used at wedding ceremonies.

7. It is made from the red flesh of imported, salted salmon, massaged between the fingers and mixed with tomatoes, crushed ice, and green onions. All these ingredients are foreign introductions.
8. Equally interesting is the fact that all the local CHT tribes wear and value similar kinds of garlands. While the Marma call the garland *Puaitha Loing Hrui*, the Chak call it *Tang Grik*; the Mro, *Keng Leng*; and the Lusai, *Cheng Thui*.
9. Monarchy, Empire, and developments in CHT: Queen Victoria: 1837–1876 = colonial annexation of Chittagong Hill Tracts; Edward VII: 1901–1910; George V: 1910–1936 = CHT becomes "totally excluded area"; George VI: 1936–1952 = 1947, partition of India, CHT becomes part of East Pakistan.
10. "After an hour of walking in the burning sun, we arrived in the village in Ruma to discover that nobody was there. They were all working the *jhum* fields and had been there since sunrise. Luckily, my local contact had a mobile number for the family and called them. However, unfortunately they had changed their minds and did not want a foreigner coming to their house. They were afraid I would bring other foreigners with me. We drank plenty of water and then set off to another village two hours away where there was another coin garland. When we finally arrived, we were exhausted and disheartened to find that again no one would meet with me. This time, I tried something different. I engaged some of the children in conversation in a mixture of Bengali and Marma, I sat on the floor and made myself small. Slowly, the elders come out to see us and out of curiosity the owner of the coin garland invited me to his house. He was not willing to part with the garland but allowed me to see it. I asked questions about the object. I explained how long I had been walking and that I felt far away from anything I recognised. Yet here on this table, there were coins with my British king on them. They laughed with me. Why did they collect coins with another king's head on? They were after all subject to their own king – the Bohmong *Raja* – but here they were wearing the coins of another king far away. They told me that these

British kings were the kings of everywhere and that the coins held great power and value as a result. My meeting with this owner drew a crowd from the village and everyone listened to the stories recounted." Field notes "Hiking Ruma hill tracts in search of a coin garland for the Horniman Museum".

11. Coins also contribute to a sense of permanence. According to Felix Martin (2014), coins survive because they are made from durable metals. They do not rust or corrode, and as a result they tend to survive the ravages of time better than most.

12. Reference to iron daggers that the British put into trade which were highly coveted and constantly affected as signs of rank.

Appendix C A toolkit to study identity on the borderlands

1. The elderly responded to this change by using imagery from local myths: "[A] buffalo is a buffalo. Even if it is raised by a lion, it will never be a lion" (Bal, 2007, p. 69).

2. The Garo community of the Garo Hills and Plains was split during partition in 1947. Those Garo that stayed in India developed in a different direction to the Garo of the hills who lived in Bangladesh and rubbed along with Bengali culture. The Garo are matrilineal and known locally as rice Christians, converting for economic betterment and education (Bal, 2007, p. 138).

3. These societies would become gift economies as they still embody the characteristics of the donor and the transactions create enduring relations of indebtedness as gifts are embedded in reciprocity.

4. According to Scott (2005), depopulation, dislocation, and the acceptance of Christianity have compounded the normal chaos of hybridity, and with it, the usual challenges to locality reproduction.

5. "As these ancestors moved into the land, they engaged in a repertoire of place-making activities: they founded new settlements, enshrined their dead, invested the land with tabus, innovated and recycled personal names attached to locales, and planted nut trees and gardens. They became one with their land, shaping it and being shaped in return into a true matrilineage with an exclusively emplaced past" (Scott, 2005, p. 206).
6. Appadurai (1986) tests a hypothesis that there is a correlation between increased uncertainty regarding ethnic identities and an upsurge in ethnic violence. No longer able to distinguish each other as too much blending between groups – physical differences are no longer clear. Dismemberment is carried out as the means "to stabilize," "to eliminate", "flux," and "to establish the parameters" of otherness (Scott 2005: 209).
7. Seeing traditional Highland dress as "a cumbrous, unwieldy habit", Rawlinson sent for a tailor who designed the philibeg or small kilt, tartan was assigned to clans, and a retail industry of epic proportions was established. Clan tartans are therefore a profitable undertaking of opportunistic woollen manufacturers (Trevor Roper, 2008, p. 199).
8. For example, Durkheim saw religion as a part of the human condition, and while the content of religion might be different from society to society over time, religion will, in some form or another, always be a part of social life.
9. "If we are to have a real comparative morphology of societies, however, we must aim at building up some sort of classification of types of structural systems" (Radcliffe-Brown, 1940, p. 6).
10. In which time is *durée* or duration.
11. A study of the complex Kachin Hill borderlands of North East Burma, based on his fieldwork between 1939 and 1943.
12. Gumsa represents the Kachin ideal of a feudal state with a ranked social hierarchy. Gumlao is a "democratic" organisation where the political entity is a single village, which, in its

extreme form, is a system of anarchic republicanism with no class differences and no chiefs.

13. "Hawaiian history often repeats itself, since only the second time is it an event. The first time it is myth" (Sahlins, 1981, p. 9).

14. Some illumination on the following definitions that are relevant to this thesis: blending is mixing that obscures individuality of each component. Coalescing is to unite to become one. Amalgam is a flexibility to change on the way to becoming mosaic. Mosaic is more fixed. Convergence also represents the process of creativity (Hymes, 2020).

References

Adnan, S. (2008). Contestations Regarding Identity, Nationalism and Citizenship During the Struggles of the Indigenous Peoples of the Chittagong Hill Tracts of Bangladesh. *International Review of Modern Sociology*, 34(1), pp. 27–45.

Ahamed, F. U. (2004). *Ethnicity and Environment: "Tribal" Culture and the State in Bangladesh*. PhD thesis. University of London.

Anderson, S. (2007). The Economics of Dowry and Brideprice. *Journal of Economic Perspectives*, 21(4), pp. 151–174.

Appadurai (1998). Dead Certainty: Ethnic Violence in the Era of Globalization. *Development and Change*, 29, pp.905–925.

Ashrafuzzaman, M. (2014). *The Tragedy of the Chittagong Hill Tracts in Bangladesh: Land Rights of Indigenous People*. Master's thesis. Lund University, Sweden.

Bal, E. (2007). *They Ask if We Eat Frogs: Garo Ethnicity in Bangladesh*. Singapore: ISEAS Publishing (IIAS/ISEAS Series on Asia).

Baron, R. (2003). Amalgams and Mosaics, Syncretisms and Reinterpretations: Reading Herskovits and Contemporary Creolists for Metaphors of Creolization. *Journal of American Folklore*, 116(459), pp. 88–115.

Barth, F. (1998) [1969]. *Ethnic Groups and Boundaries: The Social Organization of Cultural Difference*. Long Grove, IL: Waveland Press.

Barua, B. P. (2001). *Ethnicity and National Integration in Bangladesh*. New Dehli: Har-Anand Publications.

Barua, D. M. (2019). Thrice-Honored Sangharaja Saramedha (1801–1882): Arakan-Chittagong Buddhism across Colonial and Counter-Colonial Power. *The Journal of Burma Studies*, 23(1), pp. 37–85.

Bernot, L. (1967a). *Les Cak, contribution à l'étude ethnographique d'une population de langue loi [The Cak: Contribution to the Ethnographic Study of a Population's Language]*. Paris, CNRS, RCP n. 61, deuxième série, Monographies.

Bernot, L. (1967b). *Les paysans arakanais du Pakistan oriental, l'histoire, le monde végétal et l'organisation sociale des réfugiés Marma (Mog) [The Arkanese Peasants of East Pakistan: The history, the plant World and the Social Organisation of the Marma (Mog) Refugees]*. Paris: Mouton, deux volumes.

Bourdieu, P. and Nice, R. (1977). *Outline of a Theory of Practice / Pierre Bourdieu*. Translated by Richard Nice. Cambridge: Cambridge University Press.

Braudel, F. and Wallerstein, I. (2009). History and Social Sciences: The Longue Durée. *Commemorating the Longue Durée*, 32(2), pp. 171–203.

Cahyaningtyas, J. (2016). Inter-caste Marriage in Bali: A Gendered Analysis of Caste and Its Impact on Balinese Women. *Asian Journal of Women's Studies*, 22(3), pp. 193–207.

Chittagong Hill Tracts Commission (1991). *"Life is Not Ours': Land and Human Rights in the Chittagong Hill Tracts, Bangladesh*.

Douglas, M. (2002). *Purity and Danger: An Analysis of Concept of Pollution and Taboo*. London: Routledge.

Evans-Pritchard, E. E. (1937). *Witchcraft, Oracles and Magic among the Azande*. London: Oxford University Press.

Farrell, J. (2007–2008). An Elizabethan in Asia: Ralph Fitch, Our Most Adventurous Leatherseller. *The Leathersellers' Review*, pp. 16–18.

Feng, X. (2012). Chicken and Family Prosperity: Marital Ritual Among the Miao in Southwest China. *Studies on Asia Series* IV, 2(1), pp. 1–24.

Fox, R. (1967). *Kinship and Marriage: An Anthropological Perspective*. Cambridge: Cambridge University Press.

Gellner, D. N. and Schendel, W. Van. (2013). *Borderland Lives in Northern South Asia*. Durham, NC and London: Duke University Press.

The Government of Bangladesh (1979). The Chittagong Hill Tracts. *The District Gazetteer*.

Hamilton, F. (1825). An Account of the Frontier Between the Southern Part of Bengal and the Kingdom of Ava. *Edinburgh Journal of Science*, 3(6), pp. 201–212.

Handler, R. and Linnekin, J. (1984). Tradition, Genuine or Spurious. *Journal of American Folklore*, 97(385), pp. 273–290.

Herskovits, M. J. (1937). African Gods and Catholic Saints in New World Negro Belief. *American Anthropologist*, 39, pp. 635–643.

Hobsbawm, E. and Ranger, T. (2012). *The Invention of Tradition*. Vol. 15. Canto Classics. New York: Cambridge University Press.

Htin, K. M. (2015). The Marma from Bangladesh: A "de-Arakanized" Community in Chittagong Hill Tracts. *Suvannabhumi*, 7(2), pp. 133–153.

Hutchinson, R. H. Sneyd. (1978) [1906]. An Account of the Chittagong Hill Tracts. Calcutta.

Hymes, D. (2020). Pidginization and Creolization of Languages: Their Social Contexts. *International Journal of the Society of Language*, 2020(263), pp. 99–109.

Ikeya, C. (2013). Colonial Intimacies in Comparative Perspective: Intermarriage, Law and Cultural Difference in British Burma. *Journal of Colonialism and Colonial History*, 14(1), pp. 1–14.

Kapaeeng Foundation. (2010). *Human Rights report 2009–2010 on Indigenous Peoples in Bangladesh*. Dhaka: Kapaeeng Foundation.

Khan, A. M. (1999a). *Buddhism in Marma: The Maghs. A Buddhist Community in Bangladesh*. Dhaka: The University Press Limited.

Khan, A. M. (1999b). *Sangharaj Saramedha O Bangladesh Bauddhadharma*. Dhaka: Saugata Prakashana.

Leach, E. R. (1970). *Political Systems of Highland Burma: A Study of Kachin Social Structure*. London: University of London, The Athlone Press.

Lévi-Strauss, C. (1952a). Kinship Systems of Three Chittagong Hill Tribes (Pakistan). *Southwestern Journal of Anthropology*, 8(1), pp. 40–51.

Lévi-Strauss, C. (1969). *The Elementary Structures of Kinship*. Translated from the French by J. H. Bell and von J. R. Sturmer. Boston, MA: Beacon Press.

Lewin, T. H. (2004) [1870]. *Wild Races of the Eastern Frontier of India*. New Delhi: Mittal Publications.

Lewin, T. H. (1912) [1885]. *A Fly on the Wheel, or How I Helped to Govern India*. London: W. H. Allen & Co.

Malkki, L. H. (1995). Refugees and Exile: From 'Refugee Studies' to a National Order of Things. *Annual Review of Anthropology*, 24, pp. 495-523.

Martin, F. (2014). *Money: The Unauthorised Biography*. London: Vintage Books.

Mashreque, S. M. (1998). Politics of Kinship in a Traditional Peasant Community of Bangladesh. *Humanomics*, 14(3), pp. 45–75.

Mauss, M. (1954). *The Gift: Forms and Functions of Exchange in Archaic Societies*. Translated by Ian Cunnison with an introduction by E. E. Evans-Pritchard. London: Cohen & West.

Michaud, J. (1997). Economic Transformation in a Hmong village of Thailand. *Human Organization*, 56(2), pp. 222–232.

Mills, J. P. (1927). Report on the Chiefs of the Chittagong Hill Tracts and Proposals Regarding the Chiefs.

Mills, J. P. (1931). *Notes on a tour in the Chittagong Hill Tracts in 1926*. In: Census of India, Volume V: Bengal and Sikkim App II, pp. 514–521.

Mills, J. P. (1935). Note on the Backward Areas of British India and their Position under the Government of India Act, 1935.

Moshin, A. (1997). *The Politics of Nationalism. The Case of the Chittagong Hill Tracts, Bangladesh*. University Press.

Nasreen, J. and Togawa, M. (2002). Politics of Development: "PahariBengali" Discourse in the Chittagong Hill Tracts. *Journal of International Development and Cooperation*, 9, pp. 97–112.

Ortner, S. B. (1989). *High Religion: A Cultural and Political History of Sherpa Buddhism*. Princeton Studies in Culture/Power/History. Princeton, NJ: Princeton University Press.

Pru, T. U. (1950). Handwritten notes on history of the Bohmong family.

Radcliffe-Brown, A. R. (1940). *Journal of the Royal Anthropological Institute of Great Britain and Ireland*, 70(1), pp. 1–12.

Risley, H. R. (1891). *Tribes and Castes of Bengal*. Calcutta: Tea Districts Labour Association.

Roy, R. C. K. (2000). Land Rights of the Indigenous Peoples of the Chittagong Hill Tracts, Bangladesh. IWGIA Document No. 99. Copenhagen.

Sahlins, M. (1981). Historical Metaphors and Mythical Realities: Structure in the Early History of the Sandwich Islands Kingdom. Ann Arbor: University of Michigan. ASAO Special Publications; No. 1.

Sahlins, P. (1989). *Boundaries: The Making of France and Spain in the Pyrenees*. Berkeley, CA: University of California.

Scott, J. C. (2009). *The Art of Not Being Governed: An Anarchist History of Upland Southeast Asia.* New Haven: Yale University Press, Yale Agrarian Studies.

Shenk, M. K., Towner, M.C., Voss, E.A. and Alam, N. (2016). Consanguineous Marriage, Kinship Ecology, and Market Transition. *Current Anthropology*, 57, pp. S167–180.

Shils, E. (1981). *Tradition.* Chicago, IL: University of Chicago Press.

Sopher, D. E. (1963). Population Dislocation in the Chittagong Hills. *Geographical Review*, 53(3), pp. 337–362.

Spiro, M. (1977). *Kinship and Marriage in Burma: A Cultural and Psychodynamic Analysis.* Berkeley, CA: University of California Press.

Tapp, N. (2003). The Hmong of China: Context, Angency, and the Imaginary. Boston: Brill.

Thomas, N. (1991). *Entangled Objects: Exchange, Material Culture, and Colonialism in the Pacific.* Cambridge, MA and London: Harvard University Press.

Thomas, N. (1992). The Inversion of Tradition. *American Ethnologist*, 19(2), pp. 213–232.

Trevor Roper, H. (2008). Modern Great Britain and Europe/ La Grande-Bretagne et l'Europe modernes. *The Invention of Scotland: Myth and History.* New Haven, CT: Yale University Press.

Tsuda, T. (2015). Is Native Anthropology Really Possible? *Anthropology Today*, 31, pp. 14–17.

Uddin, N. (2010). Politics of Cultural Difference: Identity and Marginality in the Chittagong Hill Tracts of Bangladesh. *South Asian Survey*, 17(2), pp. 283–294.

Van Schendel, W. (2002). Geographies of Knowing, Geographies of Ignorance: Jumping Scale in Southeast Asia. *Environment and Planning D: Society and Space*, 20(6), pp. 647–668.

Visser, J. and Gerharz, E. (2016). Mobility Aspirations and Indigenous Belonging among Chakma Students in Dhaka. *South Asian History and Culture*, 7(4), pp. 370–385.

Wade, F. (2018). Fleas We Greatly Loathe. *London Review of Books*, 4(13), p. 1.

Recommended further reading

Bal, E. (2007). *They Ask if We Eat Frogs: Garo Ethnicity in Bangladesh*. Singapore: ISEAS Publishing (IIAS/ISEAS Series on Asia).

Barth, F. (1998) [1969]. *Ethnic Groups and Boundaries: The Social Organization of Cultural Difference*. Long Grove, IL: Waveland Press.

Brammer, H. (2016). Floods, Cyclones, Drought and Climate Change in Bangladesh: A Reality Check. *International Journal of Environmental Studies*, 73(6), pp. 865–886.

Buchanan, F. (1992) [1798]. *Francis Buchanan in Southeast Bengal, 1798: His Journey to Chittagong, the Chittagong Hill Tracts, Noakhali, and Comilla*. Michigan, MI: University Press.

Charney, M. (2002). Beyond State-centered Histories in Western Burma: Missionizing Monks and Intra-Regional Migrants in the Arakan Littoral, c. 1784–1860. In: J. Gommans and J. Leider, eds., *The Maritime Frontier of Burma: Exploring Political, Cultural and Commercial Interaction in the Indian Ocean World, 1200–1800*. Amsterdam and Leiden: KITLV Press, pp. 213–224.

Eriksen, T. H. (1993). *Ethnicity and Nationalism: Anthropological Perspectives*. London: Pluto Press.

Geertz, C. (1980). *Negara: The Theatre State in Nineteenth-century Bali*. Princeton, NJ: Princeton University Press.

Gellner, D. N. and Schendel, W. Van. (2013). *Borderland Lives in Northern South Asia*. Durham, NC and London: Duke University Press.

Gibson, T. P. (1986). *Sacrifice and Sharing in the Philippine Highlands: Religion and Society among the Buid of Mindoro*. Oxford: Berg Publishers.

Handler, R. (2002). Reinventing the Invention of Culture. *Social Analysis: The International Journal of Anthropology*, 46(1), pp. 26–34.

Handler, R. and Linnekin, J. (1984). Tradition, Genuine or Spurious. *Journal of American Folklore*, 97(385), pp. 273–290.

Hannerz, U. (1987). The World in Creolisation. *Africa* (London 1928), 57(4), pp. 546–559.

Herskovits, M. J. (1937). African Gods and Catholic Saints in New World Negro Belief. *American Anthropologist* no 39, 635–43.

Hobsbawm, E. and Ranger, T. (2012). *The Invention of Tradition*. Vol. 15. Canto Classics. New York: Cambridge University Press.

Kreft, S. and Eckstein, D. (2013). *Who suffers most from extreme weather events?* Global Climate Risk Index 2014, Germanwatch.

Lévi-Strauss, C. (1952b). Le syncrétisme religieux d'un village mog du Territoire de Chittagong [The Religious Syncretism of a Mog Village in the Territory of Chittagong]. *Revue de l'histoire des religions*, 141–142, pp. 202–237.

Pru, T. U. (1994). "A Brief History of the Bohmong Dynasty." TCI Journal *Poyongera*, Rajponnah special publication (In Bengali) Vol HI, pp. 28–37. Banderban: Khatamala.

Sahlins, M. (1981). *Historical Metaphors and Mythical Realities: Structure in the Early History of the Sandwich Islands Kingdom*. Ann Arbor: University of Michigan. ASAO Special Publications; No. 1.

Scott, J. C. (2009). *The Art of Not Being Governed: An Anarchist History of Upland Southeast Asia*. New Haven: Yale University Press, Yale Agrarian Studies.

Scott, M. W. (2005). Hybridity, vacuity, and blockage: visions of chaos from anthropological theory, island Melanesia, and central Africa. *Comparative Studies in Society and History*, 47(1), pp. 190–216.

Spiro, M. (1967). *Burmese Supernaturalism (A Study in the Explanation and Reduction of Suffering)*. Englewood Cliffs, NJ: University of Chicago/Prentice-Hall, Inc.

UNDP. (2004). Human Development Report 2004: Cultural Liberty in Today's Diverse World. New York.

Van Schendel, W. (1992). The Invention of the "Jummas": State Formation and Ethnicity in Southeastern Bangladesh. *Modern Asian Studies*, 26(1), pp. 95–128.

Glossary

Term	Language	Translation	Topic
Am waing	Burmese/ Marma	Inheritance	Kinship
Ang ley ma	Burmese/ Marma	English lady	
Arakan	Old term	Rakhaing or Rakhine	Geographical
Ava	Old term	Inwa	Geographical
Birgato	Bengali	Brightness/ candles/lights. Transition in states	Marriage
Boh	Burmese	Captain/warrior	Kinship
Chaing	Burmese/ Marma	Live in peace	Naming
Chameng Than Pwe or Mengla Tun Pwe	Burmese/ Marma	To be put on the path together	Marriage
Chug-mong-Le and gong-u-nai	Burmese/ Marma	Ancestor worship	Marriage
Chungmale	Burmese/ Marma	Chicken	Marriage
Damathat / dhammasat	Burmese/ Marma	Burmese law	Law

Glossary

Term	Language	Translation	Topic
Dao	Burmese/Marma	Sword: symbol of power	Marriage
Daw	Burmese/Marma	Oldest sister	Kinship
Duck egg	Burmese/Marma	Symbolises river spirit	Marriage
Ga	Burmese/Marma	Protection	Wedding gift
Gong-u-nai-u	Burmese/Marma	Pig offering to *nat* spirits	Marriage
Goun	Burmese/Marma	Shininess with power/brightness. Shiny also signifies education, spirituality, and money	Marriage
Goungphoung	Burmese/Marma	White cloth/hat on the head	Marriage
Hingsha	Bengali	Jealousy	Emotion
Hnaang Rey	Burmese/Marma	I am giving gold as a gift to take you as my wife	Marriage
Hpaga	Leach Kachin	Wealth items	Marriage
Iokia waing	Burmese/Marma	Male goods	Marriage
Ing Mak	Burmese/Marma	Dreams	Marriage

Term	Language	Translation	Topic
Ing Mak Praing	Burmese/Marma	Dreams tell	Marriage
Ing Thang Cho	Burmese/Marma	Marriage speaks	Marriage
Ink Mak (dream) Thui Thunk (interpret) Kyaing (book)	Burmese/Marma	Book to interpret dreams	Marriage
Irrawaddy	Old term	Ayeyarwady	Geographical
Jam patha	Burmese/Marma	Blackberry leaves	Marriage
Jhum	South Asian	Slash and burn or shifting cultivation	Agriculture
Ju	Burmese/Marma	Spikes	Wedding gift
Kheerohnejecho	Burmese/Marma	Love marriage	Marriage
Khogri	Burmese/Marma	Brother-in-law	Kinship
Khre mhyang/Cremyang	Burmese/Marma	White thread/white thread before rings. Oath bracelet/thread in our life from birth to death	Marriage
Khyong	Burmese/Marma	River	Religion

Term	Language	Translation	Topic
Khyong (river) shang (queen) ma	Burmese/ Marma	Water spirit	Religion
Kracsa Lakso	Burmese/ Marma	Chicken salad	Marriage
Kyang	Burmese/ Marma	Temple	Religion
Kyang Pwe Cha	Burmese/ Marma	River worship	Religion
Kyauw	Burmese/ Marma	Youngest	Kinship
Kyaw-chauw	Burmese/ Marma	Brightness/ candles/lights. Transition in states. Showing off wealth/ display	Marriage
La	Burmese/ Marma	Two hands	Marriage
Laarey	Burmese/ Marma	Going	Marriage
Lachung	Burmese/ Marma	Two hands (la) and something (chung) + bride wealth	Marriage

Term	Language	Translation	Topic
Lachung Pwe	Burmese/ Marma	Exchange of gifts day or wedding day. Also means holding hands ceremony	Marriage
Lachung Pwe dong	Burmese/ Marma	Eating at table	Marriage
Lak thei poi	Burmese/ Marma	*Medechar* sprinkles sacred water on fingers of couple	Marriage
Lak-Chang-Cha-Cha	Burmese/ Marma	Eating from same plate	Marriage
Lako	Burmese/ Marma	Bracelet	Wedding gift
Lan or langa	Burmese/ Marma	Husband	Wedding gift
Langajulako	Burmese/ Marma	Wedding bracelet	Wedding gift
Laphwe	Burmese/ Marma	Bride price	Marriage
Ley Chang Tamey or La Chung Sa Rey	Burmese/ Marma	Eating from the same dish	Marriage
Ley Tha hit or Lou Chani	Burmese/ Marma	Marriage ceremony/ holding hands	Marriage

Term	Language	Translation	Topic
Malaing chainga	Burmese/ Marma	Two-pronged chicken tongue: if it falls to the left, it is auspicious. If it falls to the right, it is unlucky	Marriage
Maline	Burmese/ Marma	Chicken chutney	Marriage
Mangla Tangrey	Burmese/ Marma	Chanting for wedding couple	Marriage
Maramagyi	Burmese/ Marma	Marma in Myanmar	Geography
May	Burmese/ Marma	Wife	Marriage
Mayu-dama	Leach Kachin	Marriage rules	Marriage
Medechar	Burmese/ Marma	The *medechar*, meaning prime person, is a man who is neither a widower nor a divorcee and who lives with one wife	Marriage
Megri	Burmese/ Marma	Sister-in-law	Kinship
Meri	Burmese/ Marma	Mother's brother's son	Kinship

Term	Language	Translation	Topic
Min ma waing	Burmese/Marma	Female goods	Marriage
Mong	Burmese	King	Kinship
Mui (wife) Jaung (ask for) Laarey (going)	Burmese/Marma	I want the daughter for my son	Marriage
Mya	Burmese/Marma	Wife	Kinship
Na kho criti	Burmese/Marma	Love marriage	Kinship
Nue	Burmese/Marma	Soft	Naming
Oingh	Burmese/Marma	Gift of wine	Marriage
Palang Makey Dong	Burmese/Marma	Fireshots fall into river	Religion
Pareit or Paritran Suttas (Mangala Suttra)	Burmese/Marma	Ward off evil	Marriage
Pegu	Old term	Bago	Geographical
Pong	Burmese/Marma	Transformation from dull to shine	Wedding gift
Praing	Burmese/Marma	Tell	Marriage
Prekha engyi	Burmese/Marma	Silk lunghi	Marriage
Prue	Burmese/Marma	White	Naming
Pui dong or Pui Dang	Burmese/Marma	Bamboo table	Marriage

Glossary

Term	Language	Translation	Topic
Rangoon	Old term	Yangon	Geographical
Rey	Burmese/ Marma	Become	Marriage
Rijangoh or Rijang-ow	Burmese/ Marma	Earthenware jar filled with water tied with white threads	Marriage
Roa	Burmese/ Marma	Village	Geography
Roa Yoenkhan	Burmese/ Marma	Village entry fee	Marriage
Roma	Burmese/ Marma	Aunt	Kinship
Rowa Shang ma	Burmese/ Marma	Tree spirit	Religion
San	Burmese/ Marma	Luck	Naming
Shifhaikoli	Burmese/ Marma	Traditional wine made with sticky rice kept between two banana trees	Marriage
Shotobi	Burmese/ Marma	House spirit (male)	Religion
Shotobi Pung ja	Burmese/ Marma	House spirit offering to bring blessing to the family	Religion
Shwe	Burmese/ Marma	Gold	Naming

Term	Language	Translation	Topic
Sing	Burmese/Marma	Luck	Naming
Somohada	Burmese/Marma	Inheritance laws	Law
Sword	Burmese/Marma	Symbol of power	Marriage
Tan	Burmese/Marma	Exceptional	Naming
Thami	Burmese/Marma	Skirt	Clothing
Thamuhaddha Vicchedani	Pali	Combined interpretation	Law
Thee Thak (drinks again) Haaing Thak (food again)	Burmese/Marma	Drinks and food again	Marriage
Theman Pungnah	Burmese/Marma	Decider of auspicious day for blessing	Religion
Thui	Burmese/Marma	Star + last born	Naming
U	Burmese/Marma	Oldest son	Kinship
Yofa	Burmese/Marma	Mother's brother's daughter	Kinship

Term	Language	Translation	Topic
Dowry	South Asian	Payment or goods from wife's family to husband, with an expectation that it would be paid back if divorced	Marriage
Dower	South Asian	This is a gift not a loan, to protect women when widowed or divorced. Traditionally it is gifted by a husband or his family, to a future wife	Marriage
Bride wealth	South Asian	These are marriage payments from the husband and his kin to the bride's family in order to officialise a marriage	Marriage

Appendix A
Introductions and experts in the Marma community

Since I was perceived as a Westerner, and at the same time also from the region, I felt that it was important to have access to a good cross section of the community that were Marma. I sought out royal family members across the generations to hear different generational voices on the same issues. Moreover, having access to cultural experts to discuss ritual steps and meanings furthered my understanding of the community's identity-making over time.

I was introduced to the area via a young man called Shai Shing Aung who was at the time a local education officer. He not only organised my accommodation, he also organised various trips into the surrounding countryside in search of Marma objects.

Khoka Sir is a senior secondary school teacher and local historian and one of the very few Christian Marma. We met twice to discuss the history of the Marma people and about the migration waves into the area. He also presides over all Bohmong installation ceremonies.

Princess Lily (34 years) is part of the 15th Bohmong family. She is the granddaughter of the late 15th Bohmong Aung Shwe Prue Chowdhury. I met Lily and her mother at the house *puja* at my compound. Lily confided in me about her grief as she had lost her only brother in a swimming accident and her sister to a forbidden marriage with a Bengali Buddhist. Lily was working for a government institute on climate change in the CHT area at the time. Together we created a family genogram on the "15th Bohmong family" from Lily's perspective.

Prince Kai is the youngest son (33 years) of the second son of the 13th Bohmong. He is also the youngest step-brother of the current 17th Bohmong. We made a family genogram together on the "17th Bohmong family".

I met with both Kai and Lily regularly, to chat, sip tea, or eat noodles at 6 pm. While I taught them English, they helped me to expand my Marma vocabulary.

Prince Shwe Aung Prue (known as Prue) is about 58 years and is the third son of the late 15th Bohmong. He works for UNDP in the CHT and was very helpful with introductions to different Bohmong families and experts on Marma culture. He lives in Rangamati, so I talked to him occasionally, but especially when I needed some distance and guidance on how to approach the royals of Bandarban.

Prince Nue Shwe Prue (46 years) is the youngest son the 14th Bohmong. He is a historian and has travelled many times to Myanmar. I worked with him intensively in December 2013 to contextualise the Marma people and to write up the history of the Marma migration story.

The Brigadier (60 years +) is also a prince. His father was the son of wife number three of the 13th Bohmong. The Brigadier was the eldest son of three brothers and one sister (Jessie's mum). He had a great collection of photos on his wall, and also some handwritten letters and notes that he had inherited from his uncle – U Tan Prue, who was the eldest son of the first wife of the 13th Bohmong. U Tan Prue was educated in the UK and decided to leave the region during the partition of India in 1947 to become an engineer in Rangoon in Burma.

I had some contact with Princess Nelly, who worked on local gender issues and the Human Rights Commission. Through her, I came to understand much about how tribal women were being treated in Bangladesh. However, since she was blacklisted by the local police, I was advised to keep my distance as I would probably be asked to leave the region if I became too involved with her local politics.

I also regularly consulted two head monks – one royal monk at the *kyang* (temple) patronised by the royal family, and one monk who was called the "people's monk" at the neighbouring *kyang*. Through them, I slowly came to understand more about Buddhism, its role in this community, and what practices are specific to this group of people. I collected data from monks at three pilgrimage sites in Bandarban district. These sites were specifically visited by Marma people from all over the hill tracts: *Khyangwa Kyang* in Bandarban; *Ching Mrong Kyang* in Ching Mrong Kaptai; and *Rowangchori Kyang* in Rowangchori. It was said that these three temples housed relics from Myanmar that came to this region with the first wave of Marma migration.

I met with the marriage experts or elders at Mro Chyang (Bamboo Stream) village: Headman Chimie Dulupara was in charge of the village of over 240 families engaged in *jhum* and cotton cultivation; Thui Mong was a 60-year-old farmer; Pijn Shwe Thui (Flower Gold Youngest) was a 76-year-old astrologer and a monk in Mandalay for approximately five years; San Aung Prue (Standard Victory White) was 65 years old and a *medechar*; and Aung Kyaw Chauw (Victory and Famous) was 36 years old and a master builder of pagodas.

I conducted interviews around the coin garland in rural areas: one with a widow and one with a family whose wife was very ill (interview Sathowing Aung). I also negotiated the purchase of a tribal bracelet from Uyoing Ching, who was 55 years old. The bracelet was called *Langajulako*: *lan* (husband), *ga* (protection), *ju* (spikes), *lako* (bracelet). The bracelets were made for a young bride, and they served the function of protecting her from beatings from her husband.

Appendix B
Historical timeline

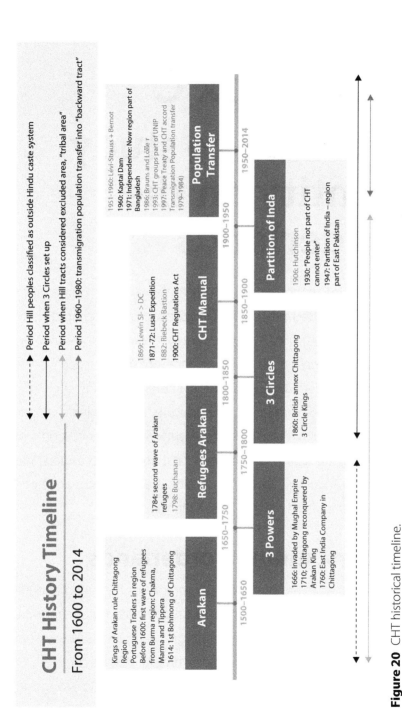

Figure 20 CHT historical timeline.

Appendix C
A toolkit to study identity on the borderlands

Studying the identity of groups in complex and fluid borderlands can be a daunting prospect! The purpose of this chapter is to outline in broad strokes the argument for the role of anthropology in understanding the lived experience of communities on the borderlands. Here are some of the theories from sociology and anthropology that provide insights into studying ethnic identities in fluid regions of the world. By using not one but different theoretical lens, I will demonstrate how to understand the many processes behind the creation and maintenance of a unique identity such as that of the Marma.

Understanding borderlands

Hilly borderlands are often remote regions of the world and act as the boundaries between more than one state. Borderlands are often geographically closer to a foreign nation and far away from the centre where their own government resides. Borderland communities can be many small "kingdoms" living alongside, interacting, and negotiating with each other. As a result, they can be familiar with different types of power and may know more than one language to help them in their daily interactions with the "other".

In *The Art of Not Being Governed* (2009), James Scott describes borderlands as "shatter zones":

> On a time-lapse photograph, these pulses of migration might look like a maniacal game of bumper cars, with each new pulse exerting its own jolt on earlier migrants and they, in turn, resisting or moving into the territory of still earlier migrants. It is this process that has created "shatter zones" and that goes a long way toward explaining the crazy quilt pattern of constantly reformulated identities and locations in the hills.
>
> (Scott, 2009, p. 329)

As part of exerting control over these shatter zones, or zones of refuge, the state – the government, the society at large or the "norm" to which the borderlands are adjacent – often defines borderland identities and, during the process, reveals its attitude towards the people who live there. The people of the borderlands can be seen as wild, close to nature, backward, in need of development, and barbarians. They are capable of eventually becoming civilised by undergoing the civilising process that the state has to offer. While the state may attempt to incorporate and absorb the peoples of the borderlands, these communities may also try to keep the state at a distance in order to continue to enjoy their freedoms.

Ethnic groups that live in the CHT can negotiate life in the shatter zones in different ways: they can assimilate to dominant state culture, temporarily align and speak as one group, or they can strongly differentiate themselves from other ethnic groups through, for example, language, history, and material objects.

The historian and sociologist Willem van Schendel explores the purposefulness of groups who live in the CHT as they define their own identity in relation to the state. He claims that the groups living between Bangladesh and Myanmar have a choice of adopting one of two competing models which are simply different because of language and cultural orientations (Van Schendel, 1992, p. 106). The first of these is a South Asian model that is Bengali and which the Chakma group have adopted as they speak and dress in the Bengali way. The other is a Southeast Asian model which is Burmese/Arakanese and Buddhist in origin and represented by the Marma. This model can be seen in the choice of words and labels: the word "Marma" signifies that the group gravitates towards the Burmese model and they use Burmese words for their leaders such as "po-mang" or "Bohmong" ("great captain"). The linguistic element of the model seems to be determined by a group's historical trading relations and trading routes: the Chakma traded with Bengalis in the Chittagong plains and therefore speak Chittagonian Bengali, while other groups in the CHT traded with the Arakanese in the south of Burma and speak dialects of Burmese. Thus, while borderland communities are defined from afar by the state, these groups can also define their own identities from within the region.

When ethnic groups assimilate

The Marma people have maintained core cultural practices in the fluid borderlands. The group's practices seem to run contrary to the choices made by their neighbours in the CHT, who have slowly assimilated to the culture of the nation state.

Shortly after independence in 1971, the new state of Bangladesh and the nation's founder – Sheikh Mujibur Rahman – claimed that the unifying features of the nation should be culture and language. Indigenous groups, seen as ethnic non-Bengalis, were seen to be lagging behind Bangladeshis and were urged to assimilate to the national mainstream to overcome their "backwardness" (Visser and Gerharz, 2016, p. 370). Ellen Bal's monograph (2007) on the Garo of the Northern Bangladesh–India border reveals the Garo response to this state policy. While the elderly Garo stay in the hills and do not worry about losing their identity,[1] the young Garo have moved to urban centres of Bangladesh and have been forced to negotiate their identity. In these urban areas, the young Garo experienced a dilution of their culture as a result of mixing with Bengalis and were aware of a process of reinventing their identity as they assimilated to Bangladeshi culture.[2]

Here's another example of what might be called the "typical" response to assimilation. The Chakma people form the largest group in the CHT and are often seen to be the group that has most assimilated to Bengali culture.

Barua (2001) claims that the Chakma assimilation process started when the early Chakma chiefs took on the Muslim title of Khan under the Mughals. Then, between 1855–1873, the Chakma queen took on the Hindu name of *rani* (queen) and, at the same time, Hindu gods were worshipped as the Hindu Bengali religious model was appropriated (Barua, 2001, p. 31).

In more recent times, the Chakma have been associated with Bangladeshi culture due to changes in their environment and new government incentives to assimilate. Visser and Gerharz's study (2016) between 1999 and 2000 revealed Chakma aspirations to attain education and that this had increased immediately after the construction of the Kaptai dam, which brought land scarcity and armed conflict to the CHT. A clause in the CHT Peace Accord supported a quota system for "tribals" in government services and educational institutions. This resulted in the migration of Chakma students and their immersion in the culture of Dhaka and other major urban centres. Another observation in Visser and Gerharz's study shows how the Chakma lower classes made up around 70 per cent of the migrants who worked in the garment industry on the outskirts of the major cities in Bangladesh (Visser and Gerharz, 2016, pp. 370–376).

The Chakma people, displaced by a loss of their Chakma lands, are an example of continual adaption and assimilation to state power in the region: from the Mughals to Hindu rulers in the past, to the Bangladeshi State more recently.

While some borderland groups assimilate, others respond to inter-ethnic contact and interdependence by accentuating their distinctness.

Creating cultural boundaries

There is a commonly held view that cultures that intermingle will always have permeable boundaries. In contrast, the cultures left in relative isolation will generate strong boundaries for themselves. However, in *Ethnic Groups and Boundaries* (1969), Frederik Barth challenged these ideas. He posited that when cultures come into contact with other cultures, boundaries tend to be drawn around selected characteristics of the group. This selection process creates separation, which in turn helps to define the group for themselves and for others. Barth writes:

> [C]ategorical ethnic distinctions… entail social processes of exclusion and incorporation whereby discrete categories are maintained despite changing participation and membership in the course of individual life histories.
>
> (Barth, 1969, pp. 9–10)

A group maintains its identity by determining criteria for membership and ways of signalling membership and exclusion on the boundaries of culture. In effect, Barth sees distinct identities and traditions arising out of contact and opposition to others, and not only because of isolation.

Hybridity: Multicultural unities

Moving away from theories that tackle differentiation on the boundaries of culture, this section will shift the focus away from the processes on the boundaries of culture to the processes that create the content of culture from within groups.

When more than one ethnic group rub alongside each other, they can join together around an emblematic ethnic value to form a hybrid group. These same societies can see themselves as unified while at the same time being plural or having multicultural unities within the unity. The concepts of creolisation, entanglement, and hybridity describe another aspect of plurality, where there is an integration of subgroups into one group. There is a fusion of different languages, and the amalgamation of elements from different cultures to create one society. Moreover, the concepts provide insights into how groups are constantly changing from within to respond to the needs of the external environment, differentiating the overall group on the Barthian boundaries of culture.

Creolisation

The idea of creolisation originates from linguistic theory in which a new language such as Yiddish and Creole is created from two different languages. The process of creolisation engages both the past and present through the ongoing reinterpretation of form and meaning of the past, as it is remade into something new (Baron, 2003, p. 112). As an approach, the deployment of the concept represents a cultural framework for understanding how new cultures are created from the conjunction of two or more cultures that come into contact.

Entanglement

In *Entangled Objects*, Thomas (1991) develops Barth's ideas of selection, integration, and differentiation by arguing that people are never the passive subjects of pure cultures. Rather, human actors adapt and change social contexts in relation to external others, incorporating some of those values and rejecting others as societies shape their own singularly entangled history. To illustrate this, Thomas examines "entangled objects", which are foreign artefacts of material culture that have been appropriated by indigenous people and incorporated within a framework of local meanings. As societies combine elements of other societies through a system of relationships, those societies can merge together. Thomas also points out that if both material culture and the economy is entangled between two societies or cultures, people will have a correspondingly creolised consciousness,[3] even if this consciousness is deeply hidden. Thomas therefore argues that "cultures" construct ethnicity when they come into contact or tension with outsiders. And that, internally, beneath the level of ethnicity, societies are cosmopolitan spaces of entanglement.

Syncretism

During migration, ethnic groups will either carry over or discard cultural elements of the group as they reach their new home. This process is called "syncretism". It was a term coined by Herskovits when analysing West African voodoo in Haiti. Herskovits studied retention and transformation of African cultural elements with new contact in the Americas. He saw that the closer a cultural group travelled to the so-called New World, certain elements of Voodoo were maintained and elaborated upon, while other elements fell away. Additionally, when there is nothing familiar in the new context, cultural traits that are more dominant are carried over into new cultural contexts and reinterpreted in light of their new surroundings. In the case of the settled Americas, African religions were carried over and reinterpreted in this way, while African cultural elements of kinship and social structure were lost. Herskovits' syncretism not only contained "survivals" from an African past, specifying the degree to which diverse cultures had integrated, but also offered a way of uniting the past with the present. The overall effect of Herskovits' theory is to highlight adaptation, assimilation, and the reconciliation of cultures with the external in the process of creating a new unique identity.

Thus, syncretism is a useful lens to understand how migration away from home towards a new land can trigger adaption or selection of internal characteristics to help the migrating group respond to new settings.

Models of chaos

Michael Scott (2005) provides another important set of tools to understand how groups of people may come together to create a hybrid group as they create a foothold in new or modern contexts. In hybrid cultures, Scott sees an oscillation between separation and integration in response to changes in the environment, and new ones – aspirational, incomplete, and competing – are constructed from selected old and new elements as hybridity elements are reconfigured.

By way of example, Scott offers two ethnographies in which he illustrates this transition from "hybridity as the universal condition of chaos" (Scott, 2005, p. 213) to cultural order-making, both of which chime with the process observable in the Marma community.

Scott introduces the concept of chaos in locality. He gives the example of the Arosi of the Solomon Islands,[4] who move from the coastal areas to the unsettled and unused "virgin forest" – *wabu* – of the interior (Scott, 2005, p. 206). These new areas of semantically empty land are seen as areas of chaos that trigger "place-making" activities that help to make the area feel safe enough to settle in.[5] The separation from all that is familiar, to settle in new lands, stimulates the integration of the subgroups into one unified entity.

Another of Scott's case studies on cultural hybridity describes the chaos that comes with blocked bodies (Appadurai, 1998)[6] or body maps (Liisa Malkki, 1995). Based on the violence of the 1972 massacres of Hutu by Tutsi in Burundi, Scott sees the violence of dismemberment as a response to a perception that it was no longer possible to distinguish Hutu and Tutsi as a result of the blending between the two groups. For example, Tutsi women, who were frequently the wives and mistresses of Hutu men and the "potential mothers of ethnically anomalous children" were considered "liminoid beings" (Scott, 2005, p. 212). Tutsi women were therefore considered to potentially contain the chaos of obstruction as partners in an inter-ethnic marriage. The case study claims that both the Rwandan Hutu on Tutsi killings of 1994, as well as the earlier Burundi massacres, restored the orderly flow of life-giving forces through the separation of pure categories that had been blurred (Scott, 2005, p. 209). In this case study, chaos is thus understood as insufficient differentiation between groups.

There is plurality in the perceptions of what constitutes chaos, as well as many techniques of re-parsing it during the process of order-making. Scott therefore argues for the Arosi and the Rwanda region that identity reverts to forms of separateness, distinctness, and difference in times of crisis.

A recap

To conclude, each theorist treats hybridity differently. Theories of creolisation, entanglement, syncretism, and the model of chaos reveal the processes involved in the integration of subgroups into one group while differentiating the overall group on the Barthian boundaries of culture. The theories provide insights into how groups are constantly changing from within the group according to the needs of the external environment. All of the processes described by the authors in this section have relevance to the Marma cultural and ethnic trends and the book will draw upon some of these approaches pragmatically at different junctures in the study.

The invention of tradition and culture

So far, the theories covered are useful in understanding processes of differentiation between groups in close contact and the internal reconfigurations that help define groups in opposition to "the other". Taken alone, however, these concepts do not explain how the structures of some communities are able to appear unchanging over time – both externally and to their inhabitants. What if processes of identity-making are able to absorb other cultural elements and strengthen boundaries, adapting to change and instability while maintaining a core set of processes that transmit and endure? To slowly move to the formation of a singular identity even as significant incorporation passes unnoticed. To answer these questions, I will now look at the internal processes that govern the invention of tradition and culture within a group, which in turn contribute to a group's journey from hybridity to singularity and the creation of an essential unchanging core of identity.

Invention of tradition

> Traditions which appear or claim to be old are often quite recent in origin and sometimes invented.
>
> (Hobsbawm and Ranger, 2012, p. 1)

Where a strong ethnic identity exists, a group's culture often appears to be rooted in traditions that are handed down, considered sacred and binding, and therefore are both unchanged and unchangeable. However, historical analysis usually shows that while some content has been transmitted over long periods, traditional forms are often invented rather than received, and re-invented in accordance with contemporaneous needs, circumstances, and creative urges.

The central argument for the invention of tradition is that (a) traditions claim to be unchanged; but (b) are not; and (c) this fact tends to go unnoticed. Thus, traditional customs change while being represented as unchanging. To illustrate their ideas, Hobsbawm and Ranger use a visual concept of a legal wig or robe to represent the invariance of tradition, which can be inflexible to unforeseen contingencies. Alongside this, custom – represented by judges – allows for the possibility of flexibility while adhering to precedent, since judges can bring about change by adapting rules to new cases without precedent.

In addition, any social practice that is carried out repeatedly will tend to develop a set of conventions and routines. So it is not only through invention and re-invention of tradition that change to culture can occur, but adaptation can also happen through customs and conventions. This is especially true when an existing use needs continuing in new conditions, and therefore must be reconfigured to these new conditions in order to operate. Or when materials in the past are revisited and new traditions are grafted onto old ones. Tradition is therefore constantly, periodically, imperceptibly, and cumulatively manipulated to keep up with change, and agency is important in making this possible.

Since change can promote both anxiety and a need for solid continuity, invented traditions can also be adaptive strategies for societies undergoing rapid change as they build bridges to a suitable past, creating the illusion of solidity within transitional environments. Of course, people can also assert continuity of tradition not only because environments are unsettled but also because they simply insist upon the value of tradition in a changing environment.

Of relevance to the CHT communities is that invented traditions can also provide an anchor in identity for communities that have been pulled into the political or cultural orbit of a more powerful society. For example, Trevor-Roper (2008) illustrates this in a case study on Scottish history and myth-making. He studies how Scottish clans respond to the encroachment of English political power and culture. There was an invention of a number of myths across Scottish history, one of which was the myth of ancient kilts and tartan. Trevor-Roper points out that kilts were not ancient but developed in the eighteenth century by an English industrialist, Thomas Rawlinson.[7] Nevertheless, "the replacement of history by myth" was an invention that rooted people's identity in the essential nature of Scottishness (Trevor-Roper, 2008, p. 14). Though they are fabrications, these traditions encompass images, cultural values and longings, and enough elements of a "real" past to meet important emotional needs of the present as well as fulfil ideological positions. Moreover, the density and durability of myths reveals how myth-making has often nothing to do with reason or evidence and everything to do with power, profit (the woollen trade), and legitimacy as they cash in on the apparent continuity of tradition.

Hobsbawm and Ranger (2012) and Trevor-Roper (2008) seem to accept the contradictions of an invented tradition as a bounded idea or entity with a core of unchanging ideas and customs that is nevertheless regularly adapted to match contemporary circumstances. But, despite these adaptations, the traditions are still imagined as unchanging.

Invention of culture

Handler and Linnekin in *Tradition, Genuine or Spurious* (1984) see tradition as an object that can change, but they also ask this question: if it does change, has it become something new or different?

Handler and Linnekin demonstrate their ideas through an analysis of the national and ethnic identification of the Quebecois. Quebecois identity is an ongoing interpretation of the past, and therefore also an invention. For example, folklore and folk dances are not fixed culture but reinterpreted continuously, and during the process, are selective as only certain items are chosen to represent traditional national culture at any given time, and other aspects of the past are ignored or forgotten.

> [T]hose elements of the past selected to represent traditional culture are placed in contexts utterly different from their prior, unmarked settings. A family

> party presented on stage, or a child's toy immured in a museum, are not, in these new contexts, quite the same things that they were in other settings; juxtaposed to other objects, enmeshed in new relationships of meaning, they become something new.
>
> (Handler and Linnekin, 1984, p. 280)

For Handler and Linnekin, ongoing cultural representations refer to or take account of prior representations, and in this sense, the present has continuity with the past. Handler and Linnekin's theory of tradition encompasses both continuity and discontinuity – with the balance in favour of discontinuity – in the attribution of new meaning in the present through reference to the unchanging past. Handler and Linnekin therefore shift the view of seeing tradition as a fixed object to a process of thought.

Inversion of tradition

Another contribution to the debate on invention of tradition is Thomas' (1992) proposition that what counts as tradition can be an inversion of previous iterations of culture. Thomas asks against what or who are traditions invented:

> I explore the ways in which the recognition of both others and selves made particular practices or customs emblematic; different encounters produced different referents for what was characteristic of a place or a people.
>
> (Thomas, 1992, p. 214)

As Barth proposed, Thomas claims that difference is created through contact with the other, not only at the level of boundary-making but also within culture itself and that culture can be further inverted in response to impositions by, for example, the colonising other. An example would be if the colonial power imposes an agenda of modernisation, groups could respond with a counter assertion of "tradition" (Thomas, 1992, p. 215). This counter-concept could then be inverted again if the colonial power in the next conjuncture imposes a traditionalist agenda, in which case indigenous groups may counter-assert an anti-traditionalist modernising agenda. For example, a term of address such as "primitive" is liable to be seized upon and inverted, or otherwise responded to, in a way that produces a new kind of self-recognition.

A recap

These perspectives on invented traditions and culture demonstrate how encounters with forces outside a community can push societies to differentiate themselves through inventions or inversions that can be continuously or periodically reinvented. From these vantage points, we can see how customs and traditions can change over time as conventions are adjusted to meet new needs, all the while maintaining an essential core. Moreover, these approaches remind us to focus on elements of change, even as Marma participants themselves direct attention, by and large, to what remains unchanged.

The reproduction and transformation of culture

To better understand how the core of a group's tradition, culture, and identity is reproduced in ways that maintain boundaries and set the group apart in spite of hybridisations and inventions, it is necessary to consider an alternative grouping of anthropological literature. In its premise and focus, the literature in the next section shifts the balance away from discontinuity within tradition to continuity within change. In this way, it may be possible to understand how core processes are able to endure in contexts of change and instability.

Here we will look at anthropological approaches that focus on the role of structures in the reproduction of culture and the various ways agency can work within stable structures to enact change over time.

The role of structure

There are many traditional sociological and anthropological theories that explore how "traditional" societies create a sense of stable equilibrium. Durkheim's (e.g. 1995 [1912]) functionalism in the late eighteenth century examined parts of a society that work together to make a functioning whole, creating a sense of equilibrium or stasis.[8] Radcliffe-Brown's functionalism saw societies as if they were classifiable species out of time and space, fixing static society in an ethnographic present.[9] However, functionalism as a theory did not adequately address the dynamic processes at work between the structures that make up the functioning whole or the generative processes that contribute to the overall stasis of the society or its ability to bring about change. For example, in *The Gift* (1954), while acknowledging the stability of structures, Mauss also detects that there are processes behind it.

> When the paths of Polynesian gifts are traced, a stable, hierarchical structure is revealed. It is not the competitive potlatch, but it is still a total system of gift. Where does the system get its energy?
>
> (Mauss, 1954, p. xii)

Lévi-Strauss (1969) and many others (e.g. Mauss, 1954) examined this energy or the processes within a system by applying the concept of "Saussaurian" linguistics to structures. Employing the lens of structural linguistics, a structural theory was developed in anthropology that covered the processes between unconsciously held mental schemas or rules (grammar) and the fluid enactment of those rules in social life (speech). The theory allows for an analysis of a society with durable structures – analogous to an unchanging grammar – with transforming practices over time such as a succession of speech events.

In structuralist approaches of this kind, variations appear to be stored up in structure similar to a charge stored up in a battery, and speaker-actors have the ability to work within the rules of structures to release the charge. On releasing the charge, processes either uphold structure or refine it to reflect the changes in the environment, while the overarching structure appears the same. An example of the latter would be the way in which Marma social structure or the structures of the Marma worldview are like the rules of chess, and Marma adaptations to changing circumstances are akin to different gambits or strategies within the rules of the game. In this way, the propensity for change is possible while structures appear stable.

The role of agency

An important aspect of structural process is the role of actors or agency as these forces purposefully work on structures to meet the demands of change in the environment, adapting them and sometimes transforming them in the process.

An important core challenge for anthropology and the social sciences is to understand the relationship between structure and agency. Structure refers to the complex and interconnected set of social forces, relationships, institutions, and elements of social structure that work together to shape the thought, behaviour, experiences, and choices of people. In contrast, agency is the power people have to think for themselves and act in ways that shape their experiences and life trajectories. Agency can take individual and collective forms.

Various theorists have studied the significance of agency by highlighting the multi-layered aspects of the concept.

In *Outline of Theory of Practice* (1977), Bourdieu describes *habitus* as "internalised structures" and "schemes of perception" that structure the agent's (shared) world-view and their "apperception" of the world in which they suppose they exist (Bourdieu, 1977, p. 86). Bourdieu's *habitus* determines action but not mechanically: conditioned actors always possess a degree of freedom in how they materialise the structural message, so there is also an improvisatory property to *habitus*. Thus, structures shape people's practices, but also people's practices constitute and reproduce structures and actors can improvise and transform previous structures, all the while conforming to the sedimented rules of the *habitus*. Thus, for example, values can be culturally and symbolically reinterpreted and re-legitimised through an interplay of agency and structure.

For Bourdieu, therefore, structure is a process and not a steady state with historical agents' thoughts, motives, and intentions being constituted within the structures by the cultures and social institutions into which they are born. This is the idea of performativity: that the materialisation of structures occurs through the improvisation of actors who singularise outcomes. Agents therefore have the capacity to engage in discerning and strategic actions such as gift exchange or marriage strategies, since they are knowledgeable actors.

Structure in reproduction and transformation

There are theories that combine structure with agency in its different forms to show how structure can be reproduced over time and transformed. The approaches covered next employ historical perspectives to uncover complex, socio-economic, and politically embedded processes of long-term structural formation and change.

The historical *longue durée*

Why are studies of the long run or *longue durée* important to understand these processes? In 1958, following on from Marx and the first social models on the basis of the historical *longue durée*, Fernand Braudel studied the relationship between agency and environment over the *longue durée*.[10] Braudel saw that the *longue durée* was not eternal but had a beginning and an end, and by viewing societies in this way, it would be possible to see what happened to structures over time. He also noted that structures that could not be adapted would eventually cease to exist.

> Certain structures, in their long life, become the stable elements of an infinity of generations. They encumber history and restrict it, and hence control its flow. Other structures crumble more quickly. But all structures are simultaneously pillars and obstacles.
>
> (Braudel, 2009, p. 178)

Kachins of Burma

Edmund Leach in *Political Systems of Highland Burma* (1970)[11] explores how individual and lineage agency transforms societies in the Kachin Hills of Burma. Leach took a *longue durée* perspective by surveying 150 years of historical records from the region to examine the Kachins at the beginning and at the end of their social cycle.

Leach discovered that the communities in the Kachin Hills at the beginning of the social cycle were gumsa (hierarchical). When the chief was overthrown, the gumsa society became more gumlao (egalitarian).[12] Leach described this as a long-phase political oscillation of tendencies towards one pole to another and that structures change from small to large and then break down into smaller ones, and that this process allows for structural variation (Leach, 1970, p. 6).

Cook's visit to the Hawaiian Islands

In *Historical Metaphors and Mythical Realities* (1981) Marshall Sahlins also deploys the idea of the *longue durée* in his account of the historical reproduction of Hawaiian social and ritual processes but also focusses on discrete events that triggered processes of cultural reproduction and transformation. Sahlins interpreted the events around Captain James Cook's visit to the Hawaiian Islands in the late eighteenth century in Hawaiian terms. He claimed that Cook appeared as a specific Hawaiian god because of the direction and time of his arrival, and that he was the only one of the Europeans who appeared god-like. Cook was associated with the fertility god Lono in the ritual cycle by the priests and incorporated into local cosmology, killed (again as Lono), and his bones kept.[13]

> Through the appropriation of Cook's bones, the *mana* of the Hawaiian kingship itself became British. And long after the English as men had lost their godliness, the Hawaiian gods kept their Englishness. Moreover, the effect was to give the British a political presence in Hawaiian affairs that was all out of proportion to their actual existence in Hawaiian waters, since they were rapidly displaced in the vital provisioning and sandalwood trade by the Americans.
>
> (Sahlins, 1981, p. 7)

The next king – Kamehemeha – inherited Cook's murder and thus the *mana* and embarked on a policy of friendship and exchange with the British and other visitors. He adopted signs of European civilisation such as table manners and clothing. Subsequent rulers saw King George IV of Britain as a "brother". The Hawaiians had therefore approached and appropriated Cook through the lens of their dominant ritual tradition of that time and killed him as part of this same traditional cycle, but also, strikingly, acquired Englishness as a result and were changed (or, at least, the chiefs were!).

Cook's appropriation as the Hawaiian fertility god Lono is a distinctive change for Hawaiians but it also represents continuity within structures of their *longue durée*. In Sahlins' study, there is agency on structures in the sense that actors find themselves replicating old structures in new circumstances. For example, when Captain Cook appears, the Hawaiians have to decide whether he is Lono or not, and when they decide that he is, he is absorbed in the cycle of repetition and reproduction. Sahlins' study reveals how a creative application of pre-existing cultural categories and schemes of practice to new encounters leads to unforeseen consequences but, in the end, a revaluation of their own cultural concepts resulting in some transformation within continuity. In this work, Sahlins is interested not only in how events are ordered by culture, but how, in that process, culture is reordered and transformed.

Structures are reproduced in the *longue durée* for both Leach and Sahlins with agency exerted within the rules of structure, either as part of practice theory or structured variation but ultimately in continuity with an essential core that transmits through time. While Leach and Sahlins privileged the role of agency in absorbing and adapting new elements to ensure stable structures, what if agency is able to do more than reproduce and adapt structures and actually transform them?

The first celibate Buddhist monastery

Sherry Ortner's *High Religion* (1989) agents have more freedom to make choices and to work within culture to enact real change while also occupying places in the structures of the *longue durée*.

Central to this is the idea that, when pushed to almost collapse, structures can also offer up choices to people.

Ortner starts with a pivotal transformative point in Nepali Sherpa history as Khumbu oral histories recount how individuals adapted structures in the building of the first celibate Buddhist monastery. Before this, the Sherpas practised folk Buddhism and priests were able to marry. The first celibate monastery was therefore something new: a new institution with its own rules, organisation, values, and ideals. Once set up, a radically new process was set in motion as monks upgraded popular religion, bringing it in line with monastic values. Therefore, the building of the celibate monastery had a far-reaching impact on Sherpa society – the structures were transformed.

Ortner is interested in the agency behind this transformation: precisely how the monastery was founded, by whom and why. What motivated the actors. How and what had been set into motion.

Ortner finds her answers in key contradictions within the structures that stimulated actors to transform it. Crucially, she discovers a significant contradiction in Sherpa inheritance rules – in recurring structures – that came to almost habitual points of collapse. On the surface, all sons inherit land and daughters inherit moveable objects. The contradiction resides in the inheritance rules of birth order, which give natural authority to some sons while none to the other sons.

> The overall effect of this contradiction – of an egalitarianism that is permanently unbalanced by a ranking principle, and a ranking principle that is

> permanently countered by an egalitarian rule – is a chronic fraternal rivalry that reappears throughout Sherpa history.
>
> (Ortner, 1989, p. 35)

As a result, some younger brothers are pushed into exile out of jealousy and the resulting praxis or shift of context enables new opportunities for those who are looking to increase their social worth.

> Reproduction takes place either because people cannot see alternatives, or do not have the power to institutionalize the alternatives that they see. Changes take place because alternatives become visible, or because actors have or gain the power to bring them into being.
>
> (Ortner, 1989, p. 201)

The contradictions in inheritance rules lead to agents working within structures to generate a certain pattern of action. Ortner draws upon an interest-theory view of actors as rationalist strategists that built the celibate monastery to increase the worth of certain individuals. And this agency on structures transformed Sherpa society. Through her study, Ortner reveals the importance of cultural mediation and reinterpretation that enable structures to transform while helping the structures to endure overall.

A recap

To summarise, all three theorists demonstrate the importance of studying structures over time to see how structures are reproduced. The Kachins exist in moving equilibrium on the borderlands while appearing to be the same and some structural variation is achieved. Sahlins' islanders work within their cultural schemas to incorporate encounters with "the other", and through a process of appropriation, they are slowly transformed as a society. In contrast, Ortner's Sherpa actors respond to and work with the structural contradictions in their inheritance rules to move to better positions within society and, in the process, instigate the transformation in values of the celibate Buddhist monastery.

In this book, we will explore Marma agency on structures, whether on marriage rules or when material culture helps the group to reproduce structures and maintain continuity within contexts of change. This kind of agency is limited to adapting and absorbing, to perpetuate and reproduce structures and the overall system.

Applying theories to the Marma

The CHT region is an area where groups have moved around and collided with each other, with dominant powers in different periods. Some populations have assimilated to other groups or dispersed, but unlike other groups in the CHT borderlands, the Marma have both asserted and cultivated a sense of ethnic singularity. The Marma people were originally a diasporic group that slowly over time became a blending, a coalescence, and an amalgam[14] of elements from different but similar groups, as singular ethnic entities were decomposed to be replaced by new configurations. Significantly, this process eventually moved this hybrid group into the direction of a more singular ethnic community.

This appendix explored different ways of understanding the processes of identity formation and the maintenance of a core of cultural practices on the borderlands, from adaptation and assimilation on the boundaries of culture as hybrid groups undergo a process of defining the group's basic characteristics in opposition to the other, to understanding the processes at work within culture through creolisation, syncretism, entanglement, and hybridity. These theorists broadly argue that distinctive culture and specific ethnicity is a cultural illusion: rather, "specific" cultures and societies are the hybrid result of much contact, mixing, diffusion, and borrowing, and that the only thing that is specific, for any given fleeting moment, is the configuration of their complex hybridity. These theories, while pointing towards a fluid process of reconfiguring and recasting of structure, essentially also point to the instability of ethnic essence.

The different approaches with similar conceptual outcomes stress that traditional practice and ethnic identity are invented afresh according to present historical contexts and in response to both internal and/or external pressures. Sometimes, cultural invention seems to strengthen singular ethnicity or invention inverts things and tradition is downplayed. Other times, through invention and selective borrowing, culture is invented, continually re-invented, and recast in the discontinuous present.

Finally, while acknowledging changes (inventions, hybridisations, impositions, and excisions) to "traditional" societies, structural approaches examine enduring structures, configurations, and scenarios that are core to the organisation of these social spheres and which underpin claims to enduring cultural distinctness and singular ethnicity. These theories cover the cultural reproduction of structures in the long run and the sometimes peripheral and sometimes central role of agency on this reproduction. The result is a cultural identity that is continuous while undergoing transformations when structures reach a point of collapse.

Employing the various ideas and approaches of this appendix, the book explored the ways in which this seemingly stable society is busy accentuating its difference to other groups in a fast-changing environment on the borderlands.

Appendix D
Royal chart and new genogram

For the preparation of genogram work (Figure 21), I made sure that materials were on hand. Pencils, rulers, markers, and a large sheet of paper were used to create new genograms: two in total. These served as discussion points with my informants, and also family secrets and taboos were captured.

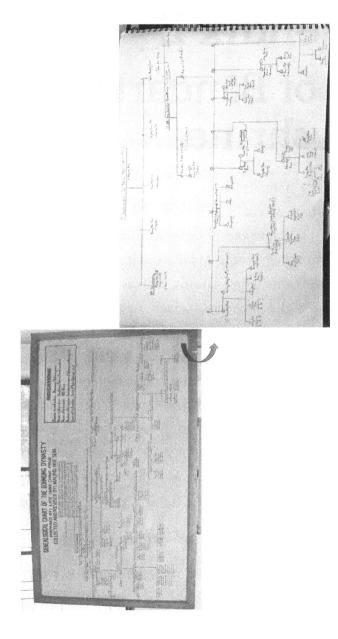

Figure 21 Royal chart up until 1997 with genogram addition from 9th Bohmong and his descendants until 2014.

Appendix E
Map of Bandarban with shrines

According to 2001 statistics for Bandarban town, there are three wards in Bandarban *puroshava* (district). Ward One constitutes the Uzani and Madyam *para* (village) with substantial ethnic populations, among which the Marma predominate by about 80 per cent, while other ethnic groups, such as the Tanchangya, Bawm, Chakma, and a few Mru families, altogether form 10 per cent and the remaining 10 per cent are Bengali. Ward Two consists of the bazaar, bus station, and court building areas and is the Bengali majority area, constituting of 85 per cent Bengali, with the rest of the population made up of different ethnic groups. Ward Three is relatively small in size. It consists of the hospital area and the *kyang* (temple) area and Bengalis constitute about 73 per cent of the population, with the rest composed of different ethnic groups. (See Figure 22.)

Map of Bandarban with numbered shrines:

1. **Champa and bodha tree near saw mill – North Chengabaan:** This is the home of the tree spirit. The 5th Bohmong was worried that the original champa tree would die so he allowed a bodha tree to grow there as well and both

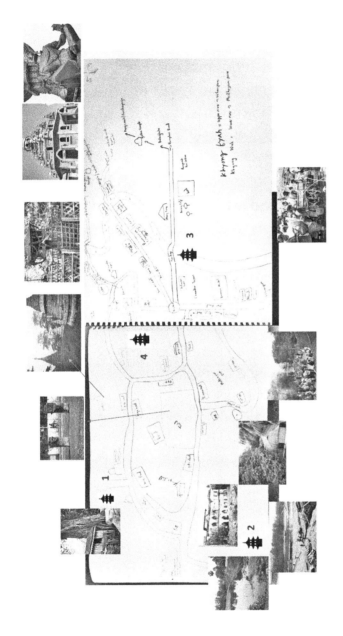

Figure 22 Map of Bandarban with shrines.

trees are now intertwined. This place is also close to the old cremation ground, between the edge of the town and the beginning of the forest.

2. **Water shrine on Sangu (West) – Ujani Ghat:** This comprises two shrine structures built from bamboo, which mark a point in the bend of the river for *kyang pwe cha* (river worship). This point is where spears and *Palang Makey Dong* (gun shots) from the other side of the river resulted in bullets falling into the waters within a specific range. The point marks the safe boundary in the river from gun shots and spears.

3. **Below bridge and to the left of Upper Ghat:** This is the point where the Marma village ends and foreign lands begin. Again, a bamboo structure in the river is built for worship.

4. **Bodha tree:** On the way to the tennis courts, to the left of the police station. Here, there is also a Bodha tree, signifying the edge of town and overlooking the valley.

Appendix F
Documentary – To Be a Marma

www.postcodefilms.com/projects/to-be-a-marma

Index

Arakan kingdom 1

assimilation 30

astrologers 56

Bandarban 2–6, 12, 33, 50, 84, 86, 104, 110–111, 117–118, 121, 123–130, 135, 140, 146, 153, 168, 172, 211–212, 246

Bangladesh War of Independence 10, 29

Bangladeshi army 4

Bangladeshi kinship 45

Barricades 62

Bengal Boundary Commission 27

'Bengalization' of the hills 29

Bohmong ix, 3–7, 9, 12, 23, 25, 32–33, 48, 80–82, 84, 102–107, 109–110, 114–120, 122–125, 127, 129–134, 137–138, 140–149, 151–152, 155–159, 172, 210–211, 218, 245–246

Bohmong Circle 6, 9, 23, 32, 80, 84, 134, 152

borderlands ix–1, 7–10, 15, 19–20, 22–23, 35–36, 42, 44, 101, 154, 163, 167, 170–171, 216–218, 241–243

bride payment 93–94

bride price 45, 51, 94–95, 98, 100, 138, 153

bride wealth 93, 138, 153, 155

British Empire 1, 27, 33, 88, 122, 130, 143–144, 156

Chakma Circle 6, 23, 32

Chakma kinship 44

Chakma people 2, 34, 36, 219–220

chickens 74–75

Cholera outbreak 124

CHT Regulations Act of 1900 25

clan exogamy 44, 48, 54, 79

climate change 7, 15–16, 197, 211

coin garlands 152–153

concept of chaos 38, 224

consanguineous marriage 46

creolization 37–39, 167, 221–222, 225, 242

customary law 31, 81–82, 85, 89–90, 92, 99, 133, 166

dowry 46, 65, 92–95, 98

dreams 58

East Pakistan 2, 10, 27–29, 153, 170

The Edict 126

elopement 45, 51–52, 54, 86, 164

entangled objects 38, 157–158, 222

ethnic endogamy 17, 80

exogamy 46, 48, 55, 63, 72–73, 99

faithful followers 104, 107

four spirit shrines 125

globalization 1

Golden Temple 6

inheritance 42, 45, 47, 52–54, 77, 80, 85–87, 89–92, 98, 100, 134, 165, 239–241

inter-ethnic marriage 80, 88–89

invention of culture 40, 229

invention of tradition 39, 226–227

inversion of tradition 40, 230

jhum cultivation 20, 148

Kaptai Dam 28

Kingly swords 141

longue durée 41, 101–102, 160, 235–236, 238

Marma marriages 54, 166

Marma women 51

marriage customs 43, 52–53, 95, 99, 164, 166

marriage payments 92–95

marriage rituals 16, 44, 54, 60, 70, 72, 76–77, 99, 128, 164

marriage rules and customs 16

material culture ix, 8, 17, 38, 42, 101, 136–139, 152, 155–157, 159–160, 164–165, 170, 222, 241

matrilocal residence 53

migration 1, 5–6, 8, 17, 19, 29–31, 34, 36, 38, 44, 48, 83, 101–102, 104, 106–107, 109, 113, 121–122, 126, 128, 134–135, 137–138, 143–144, 160, 163–165, 170, 210–212, 217, 220, 223–224

Mong Circle 6, 23, 25, 32

the Mughals 1, 22–23, 33, 114–115, 219–220

nat 60, 123–127, 133–134, 139

oral histories 106, 109–110, 239

patrilineal descent 45, 47, 53, 76

Peace Accord 31–32, 34, 36, 84, 145, 220

Pegu 6

polyandry 97

Population Transfer Programme 82

the Portuguese 1, 114–115, 140

Raj Punya 145

Royal Chart 102, 104, 244–245

Royal Palace 130

Santi Bahini 31

settlement 17, 30, 47–48, 101–102, 110, 118, 121, 123, 126, 128–129, 134–135, 137–138, 160, 163–164, 168

shininess 6–7, 139–140, 151

social contract 65

stoning myth 62

structure 41, 232, 234–235

syncretism 38–39, 102, 134, 138, 159, 167, 223–225, 242

wedding day 61, 63

CPSIA information can be obtained
at www.ICGtesting.com
Printed in the USA
BVHW030554100922
646658BV00011B/994